A PiL BOOK

WEAPONS OF
DESERT STORM

Introduction and consultation by:

COL. WALTER J. BOYNE, USAF (RET.)

TABLE OF CONTENTS

F-117A Stealth

MiG-29 Fulcrum

Front cover: F-15 Eagle

Challenger

M198 Towed Howitzer

Walter J. Boyne is a retired colonel from the United States Air Force and a prominent military consultant and writer. He is former director of the National Air and Space Museum and is the best-selling author of *The Smithsonian Book of Flight, The Leading Edge,* and the forth-coming novel, *Eagles At War.*

Nimitz-class aircraft carrier

Introduction

Prelude to Desert Storm

The war that has erupted in the Persian Gulf is one of religious fervor, tribal intransigence, resentment of foreign governments, and cruel, capricious leadership. In a word, it is *exactly* like all of the wars fought in the area since the dawn of time, with one tremendous difference: In this war there has been deployed remarkably advanced technology that has the power to win with a surgical precision that is merciful to the civilian populace. *Weapons of Desert Storm* takes a close, illustrated look at more than 50 examples of this technology—American, Allied, and Iraqi weapons of the air, land, and sea.

There is no little irony that such an advanced war should be fought in the area where human history began. It was in Iraq that the earliest evidence of organized human society is found—older than any found in Egypt, a thousand years older than any found in China.

In wars that have raged across the region, most have been centered around the ancient lands drained by the Euphrates and Tigris rivers. This area, much of it inhospitable mountain or desert land, has been blessed and cursed by its intense tribal and religious loyalties, and by a susceptibility to strong-man leaders.

Arab nationalism

Throughout the 19th century and into the first decades of the 20th, Iraq was dominated by the Turkish Ottoman Empire and, later, by the British. Then, as now, great powers were beckoned to the region by oil.

By the end of World War I, Iraqi desires for self-determination became apparent; when Arab tribesmen rose up in rebellion against Great Britain in 1920, they were decisively beaten by the Royal Air Force.

Anti-British sentiment continued into the early years of World War II. A second revolution against Britain was mounted in 1941, and once again the Iraqis were defeated by the RAF.

There followed a period of relative tranquility, in which Iraq adhered so closely to the Allied line that it became eligible, in May 1941, for lend-lease assistance from America. This was the start of an almost

Below: *Iraqi antiaircraft guns fire at Allied warplanes over Baghdad, early in the Desert Storm campaign.*

CONCENTRATION OF FORCES AT OUTBREAK OF DESERT STORM

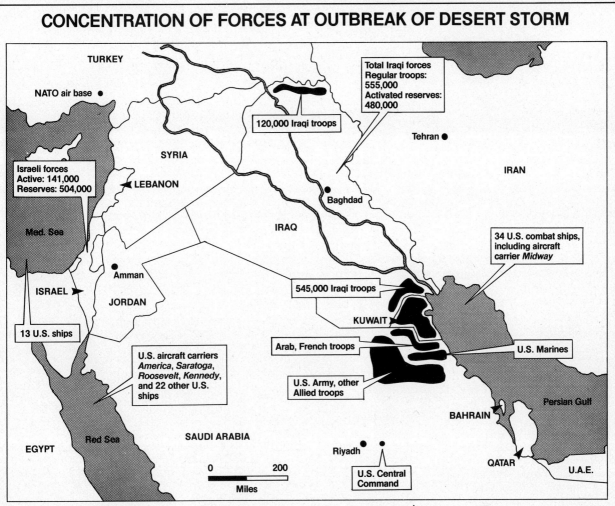

TURKEY

NATO air base ●

Total Iraqi forces
Regular troops:
555,000
Activated reserves:
480,000

120,000 Iraqi troops

SYRIA

Tehran ●

IRAN

Israeli forces
Active: 141,000
Reserves: 504,000

◄ LEBANON

Baghdad ●

Med. Sea

IRAQ

34 U.S. combat ships,
including aircraft
carrier *Midway*

● Amman

545,000 Iraqi troops

ISRAEL ►

JORDAN

KUWAIT

13 U.S. ships

Arab, French troops

U.S. Marines

U.S. aircraft carriers
*America, Saratoga,
Roosevelt, Kennedy,*
and 22 other U.S.
ships

U.S. Army, other
Allied troops

Persian Gulf

BAHRAIN

SAUDI ARABIA

EGYPT   Red Sea

Riyadh ● ●

QATAR

U.A.E.

0   200
Miles

U.S. Central
Command

unending flow of weapons,
technology, and materiel from
larger states that continued
until the late 1980s.

After a turbulent decade of
violent internal politics, yet
another revolution occurred in
July 1958. The Iraq republic
was proclaimed, a radical Arab
state committed to the cause
of revolutionary nationalism.
General Abdul Karim Kassim
became its head.

Kassim immediately asked
the Soviet Union for military
assistance, which was given
promptly and in full measure.

Right: *A dense column of smoke
rises from the Iraqi Ministry of
Defense in Baghdad following a
night of Allied bombing of the
capital city.*

Enter Saddam Hussein

Iraq in the 1960s and '70s was marked by an incredible proliferation of attempted revolutions, internal wars suppressing the Kurd national movement, and border clashes with its neighbors, particularly Kuwait and Iran. A relatively unknown revolutionist named Saddam Hussein organized a militia for the Ba'ath Party, which seized power permanently in 1968, and placed General Ahmed Hassan al-Bakr in nominal control. Saddam Hussein was actually in charge, and engineered the 1972 treaty with the Soviet Union that not only brought an increased supply of modern weapons, but served to stabilize Iraq's internal political situation.

Al-Bakr retired in 1979—an unusual occurrence for an Iraqi leader—and Saddam Hussein openly assumed control. One of his first actions was to execute 21 of his Cabinet members, many of them purportedly by his own hand.

In September 1980, Hussein sought to take advantage of the turmoil in neighboring Iran following that country's revolution, and launched what he thought would be an intense, but brief, war. Many things were at issue: religion, race, frontier disputes, and, inevitably, oil.

Saddam's decision to go to war with Iran didn't make sense when military strengths were compared. Iran's armed forces were equipped with the most modern American weapons, including F-4, F-5, and F-14 fighters, M-48 and M-60 tanks, and the latest in electronic countermeasures and communications equipment. Hussein calculated, however, that the Ayatollah Khomeini—a personal enemy of his—had so isolated himself from the west that the Iranian armed forces would be unable to function from a lack of spare parts for their weaponry. Further, Hussein hoped that his own charismatic presence would spur a revolution among the Iranians.

Instead, Iran fought back against Iraq with a bitter fanaticism, and the Iraqi *blitzkrieg* was set out to dry in the winds of the Iranian desert.

A savage stalemate followed, one far more reminiscent of the Western front in 1918 than of the mobile desert tactics of World War II. One particularly reminiscent element was Saddam's use of poison gas against not only Iranian troops and civilians, but behind the lines against the always-rebellious Kurds of his own nation.

The Iraq-Iran war lasted for eight years and cost more than 100,000 Iraqi lives. It absolutely devastated the Iraqi economy, leaving it 70 billion dollars in debt and faced with tremendous reconstruction costs.

The invasion of Kuwait

Saddam Hussein sought to reconstitute his country by invading Kuwait. In less than four hours on August 2, 1990, Iraqi tanks crossed from the border into the capital, Kuwait City, giving Hussein control of 24 percent of the world's oil supply.

Saudi Arabia was clearly Iraq's next target—and if Iraq annexed that nation, Saddam Hussein's share of the world's oil supply would jump to 44 percent. A longtime ally of the United States, Saudi Arabia immediately appealed for help.

The United States responded immediately, sending advance forces into the country, while creating the political framework within the United Nations to have Iraq denounced as an aggressor, and ordered to leave Kuwait and restore the Kuwaiti government. January 15, 1991, was eventually set as the deadline for Saddam Hussein to remove his forces from Kuwait.

Desert Storm

Hussein ignored the United Nations deadline. The Allied military buildup—Desert Shield—was followed, on January 16, 1991, by the start of Desert Storm, the Allied campaign to drive Iraqi forces from Kuwait.

Iraq's invasion of Kuwait destroyed, perhaps forever, the hopes for Arab unity and brotherhood, and resulted in the coalescence of two opposing camps. On Iraq's side are King Hussein of Jordan and Yassar Arafat of the Palestine Liberation Organization; allied against them are Hafez Assad of Syria, Hosni Mubarek of Egypt, and King Fahd of Saudi Arabia. To the west is Iran, approving of the UN sanctions, yet offering to help Iraq and potentially becoming its ally in the event of a broader war. To the north is Iraq's former conqueror, the ancient enemy Turkey.

Iraq is a small nation of some 17 million inhabitants, still suffering from the ravages of its war with Iran. From the start, it had only a faint hope of breaking up the United Nations coalition allied against it, and no hope at all of withstanding that force's military might. Regardless, Saddam went into the conflict controlling an immensely powerful land army equipped with modern tanks and artillery. He had a missile force and, reputedly, the capability and probable inclination to conduct both chemical and biological warfare. Against him was arrayed the most powerful and the most technologically advanced armed force ever deployed. In Saddam Hussein's own words, he had unleashed "the mother of wars."

Colonel Walter J. Boyne
United Stated Air Force (Ret.)

AIR WEAPONRY

Fighters, attack jets, bombers, reconnaissance planes, helicopters. All of these were brought to bear by the United States in the Desert Storm campaign against Iraq. Firmly anchored by these awesome fighting machines, the United Nations established air-superiority with blinding speed and an intensity not seen since the Middle East Six Day War of 1967. Every element of the UN forces—land-based and seaborne—functioned within a computer-like war plan that slashed through essential Iraqi

command and control installations like a knife through a jugular vein.

The mission
The initial passive resistance of the Iraqi air forces was surprising, permitting UN forces to concentrate on Iraq's greatest threat: the fixed and mobile Scud missile launchers. The fixed units were attacked early on, but the mobile units by their very nature presented a difficult target.

Allied air-superiority is exemplified by the F-14 Tomcats stationed on aircraft carriers throughout the Middle East.

United States air power faced its toughest challenge when it turned its attention to Iraqi troops, artillery, and tanks—all entrenched in desert dug-outs. There, a new chapter in combat history will be written: massive tonnages of bombs dropped by B-52s, augmented by precision strikes with smart bombs. American air power had arrived.

F-14 Tomcat

Grumman F-14 Tomcat—United States

The F-14 Tomcat—the U.S. Navy's most formidable jet fighter—has flown many sorties from aircraft carriers located in the Mideast.

The F-14 Tomcat was designed as a fleet air-defense interceptor capable of serving into the 21st century. It is the latest in a long line of Grumman "carrier cats" that date back to before World War II. Designed in the late 1960s, it was determined early on that the F-14 would be a "cat"; and since the man behind the project was Admiral Tom Connolly, then Deputy Chief of Naval Operations for Air, the new airplane was instantly called Tom's Cat. The Tomcat first flew in 1970; today, nearly 400 Tomcats are operational on U.S. Navy carriers throughout the world.

Combat-tested

The F-14 had been blooded in combat prior to operation Desert Storm. Two Navy F-14 aircrews shot down two Libyan Su-22 fighters over the Gulf of Sidra in the Mediterranean Sea on August 19, 1981, when the latter attempted to attack the aircraft carrier *Nimitz*. On January 4, 1989, two F-14 crews from the carrier *John F. Kennedy* shot down a pair of Libyan MiG-23s in the same area.

The F-14 Tomcat has variable-geometry wings that can change shape in flight to match altitude conditions and speed needs. The aircraft carries a crew of two, a pilot and a backseater who operates the complex offensive radar and weapons systems. It is armed with a 20 millimeter cannon, as well as an assortment of guided missiles such as the AIM-9 Sidewinder and AIM-54 Phoenix air-to-air missiles. The Phoenix missile was designed especially for use by the F-14.

GRUMMAN F-14D TOMCAT

Wingspan (unswept):	64 ft., 1.5 in.
Wingspan (swept):	38 ft., 2.5 in.
Length:	62 ft., 8 in.
Height:	16 ft.
Weight (maximum take-off):	74,349 lbs.
Engines:	Two General Electric F110-GE-400 turbofans
Engine thrust:	28,500 lbs.
Maximum speed:	1,734 mph
Maximum range:	2,000 miles
Service ceiling:	50,000 + ft.

F-15 Eagle
McDonnell Douglas F-15 Eagle—United States

The F-15 Eagle is to the U.S. Air Force what the F-14 is to the U.S. Navy: the leading edge of fighter technology as defined by the mission requirements of that particular service. Widely regarded as the best air-superiority fighter in the world, the F-15 demonstrated its superior capabilities above Lebanon's Bekaa valley in June 1982, when Israeli F-15s tackled the best Soviet-built fighters in the Syrian Air Force and smoked 58 of them at no loss to themselves.

The best of everything

The multi-role capability of the F-15 makes it one of the most versatile and cost effective fighters in history. The plane was designed to take everything that had been learned in air-to-air combat in Vietnam, add the best that modern emerging electronics technology had to offer, and build the best possible fighter to fulfill the Air Force mission. The first Eagles flew in July 1972, and the first F-15As entered squadron service four years later. The F-15C followed in 1979. By the early 1980s, Eagles had already begun to replace the F-4 Phantoms as the Air Force's first-line fighters. In 1987, the Air Force began taking deliveries of the F-15E, a long-range, two-seat fighter-bomber based on the F-15D.

The Eagle's armament includes a 20 millimeter cannon

A pair of F-15 Eagles on patrol. The F-15E Eagle is the Air Force's latest version of this powerful fighter.

and AIM-7 Sparrow, AIM-9 Sidewinder, and AIM-120 AMRAAM air-to-air missiles.

In addition to the United States, the F-15 is also in service in the Israeli and Saudi Arabian air forces.

McDONNELL DOUGLAS F-15C EAGLE

Wingspan:	42 ft., 9.75 in.
Length:	63 ft., 9 in.
Height:	18 ft., 5.5 in.
Weight (maximum take-off):	68,000 lbs.
Engines:	Two Pratt & Whitney F100-PW-100 turbofans
Engine thrust:	23,830 lbs.
Maximum speed:	Mach 2.5 +
Maximum range:	3,570 miles
Service ceiling:	60,000 ft.

F-16 Fighting Falcon

General Dynamics F-16 Fighting Falcon—United States

were used to attack and destroy the Iraqi nuclear plant at Osirak.

The F-16 Fighting Falcon is named after the mascot of the U.S. Air Force Academy at Colorado Springs. The idea behind the F-16 was to build a large number of lightweight, low-cost fighters to augment the squadrons of larger, more expensive F-15s. The primary F-16 assembly line is at the General Dynamics plant in Fort Worth, Texas, although it is also produced by factories in Belgium and the Netherlands. The first F-16 squadron was activated by the U.S. Air Force in 1979. F-16s have since been adapted for service in a number of NATO countries as well as Israel.

The only complaint that the pilots of the F-16 Fighting Falcon have is that there aren't enough Iraqi planes engaging in combat!

The F-16 Fighting Falcon is agile enough to dogfight and powerful enough to carry a heavy bomb load.

The F-16 Fighting Falcon saw action against Iraq prior to Desert Storm. In June 1981, Israeli F-16 fighter-bombers

The Electric Jet

The F-16 is a single-seat aircraft. Swift and agile yet capable of carrying heavy bomb loads, it may serve as an interceptor or fighter-bomber. Its control surfaces are entirely fly-by-wire, meaning that the work once done by hydraulics is now done in the F-16 by a computerized network of electric motors—hence its nickname, the Electric Jet. The Mach 2 F-16 is easy to service and has one of the lowest turn-around times in the Desert Storm theater; an engine change can be made in about 30 minutes.

The F-16 may be armed with AIM-9 Sidewinder and AIM-120 AMRAAM air-to-air missiles, and/or conventional and nuclear bombs, the AGM-65 Maverick missile, and the AGM-45 Shrike and AGM-88 HARM antiradar missiles. The F-16 is also armed with a 20 millimeter cannon.

GENERAL DYNAMICS F-16C FIGHTING FALCON

Wingspan:	31 ft.
Length:	49 ft., 3 in.
Height:	16 ft., 8.5 in.
Weight (maximum take-off):	42,300 lbs.
Engine:	One Pratt & Whitney F-100-PE-220 turbofan or one General Electric F110-GE-100 turbofan
Engine thrust:	25,000 lbs.
Maximum speed:	Mach 2
Maximum range:	2,415 miles
Service ceiling:	50,000 ft.

F/A-18 Hornet

McDonnell Douglas F/A-18 Hornet—United States

The F/A-18 Hornet evolved from the Northrop YF-17, which was rejected by the Air Force in favor of the YF-16. The Hornet is the U.S. Navy's close-in air-superiority fighter that defends aircraft carrier task forces. The Hornet is also the Marine Corps' premier attack aircraft, supporting its ground forces. Whether used by the Navy or the Marine Corps, the Hornet is the same plane; the "F" and "A" designations simply describe its role as either a fighter jet or an attack jet.

The "economical" choice

The Hornet is a small, twin-engine jet aircraft, which makes it appealing to the Navy and Marines. The F/A-18 Hornet first flew in November of 1978 but did not officially enter service until 1983.

The Hornet's armament includes a 20 millimeter cannon mounted on the top center of the nose. In its fighter configuration, the Hornet carries AIM-9 Sidewinder air-to-air missiles on wingtip racks. Other weapons, such as the AIM-7 Sparrow, are carried underwing. For attack/fighter-bomber missions, the F/A-18 Hornet's armorer can select from conventional or nuclear bombs, AGM-88 HARM antiradar missiles, AGM-65 Maverick air-to-ground missiles, and AGM-109 Harpoon antiship missiles.

In addition to the single-seat variant, the Navy has procured a two-seat Hornet variant (F/A-18C/D), which is designed to provide all-weather/night attack capabilities. The F/A-18 is also employed in Desert Storm operations by the Canadian Air Force.

The F/A-18 Hornet flies carrier air patrol missions and also provides ground support for the Marines.

The Gulf War was tailor-made to the Hornet's capabilities, stretching them to their limit, yet providing ample means to validate them. The Hornet's quick turn-around time accounts for its high sortie rate.

McDONNELL DOUGLAS F/A-18 HORNET

Wingspan:	37 ft., 6 in.
Length:	56 ft.
Height:	15 ft., 3.5 in.
Weight (maximum take-off):	36,710 lbs.
Engines:	Two General Electric F404-GE-400 turbofans
Engine thrust:	16,000 lbs.
Maximum speed:	Mach 1.8 +
Maximum range:	2,303 miles
Service ceiling:	50,000 ft.

Mirage 2000

Dassault-Breguet Mirage 2000—France

the Mirage 2000. The Mirage 2000 flew for the first time on March 10, 1978, and the first French Air Force squadron became operational in July 1984.

The Mirage 2000's delta wing increases lifting capacity and greatly improves the aircraft's low-speed, low-altitude performance. Additionally, the delta wing facilitates sharper high-speed turns at high altitudes. However, the large wing makes the Mirage 2000 a gas guzzler at low altitudes and speeds. The design is subject to a degree of instability during some phases of flight.

Fly-by-wire

Control is maintained by a computer-operated fly-by-wire system. This system automatically adjusts aerodynamic control surfaces and engine output to keep the aircraft stable.

The Mirage 2000 is a heavily armed aircraft. The nine hard point pylons (four under the wings, five under the fuselage) can carry a total of 13,890 pounds of weapons, including air-to-air and other missiles, rockets, and various bombs. The aircraft is also equipped with two 30 millimeter cannons built into the fuselage.

Although its performance as a low-altitude strike fighter is less than desired, the Mirage 2000 has proved to be an extremely successful fighter interceptor. To date, the French Air Force has purchased 273 Mirage 2000s. A total of 136 are designated the Mirage 2000C. The Mirage 2000 also flies with the air forces of Egypt, Greece, India, Jordan, Peru, and the United Arab Emirates.

The Mirage 2000 is virtually identical in appearance to earlier series Mirage aircraft—a potential problem because the Iraqi Air Force flies both the Mirage F-1 and EQ-5.

The Mirage 2000 first flew on March 10, 1978. The French Air Force began taking deliveries in 1983.

In December 1975, the French government approved the development of a new delta-wing fighter aircraft to be called

DASSAULT-BREGUET MIRAGE 2000C

Wingspan:	29 ft., 11.5 in.
Length:	47 ft., 1.25 in.
Height:	17 ft., 0.75 in.
Weight (maximum take-off):	37,480 lbs.
Engine:	One SNECMA M53-P2 turbofan
Engine thrust:	21,385 lbs.
Maximum speed:	Mach 2.26
Maximum range:	1,118 miles
Service ceiling:	59,000 ft.

C2/C7 Kfir

Israel Aircraft Industries C2/C7 Kfir—Israel

The existence of the Kfir ("Lion Cub") fighter plane had been rumored for years before it was unveiled in the spring of 1975. Since then, modifications and changes have kept the plane in the top echelon of the world's fighter aircraft.

Good handler

The Kfir is a derivative of the basic Dassault Mirage design. Among its distinguishing characteristics, the Kfir-C2 has nonretractable, removable, swept-back canards located just aft of the engine air intakes. The canards give the plane better sustained turning performance and improved direction control without excessive G forces or loss of airspeed. Wind deflectors along the side of the nose and a large delta wing further enhance the Kfir's maneuverability. Israel Aircraft Industries claims these modifications also enhance takeoff and landing performance by reducing the length of runway needed.

The Kfir-C7 is an up-rated version of the original Kfir-C2. The C7 model has higher thrust ratios, two additional hard points for weapons or external fuel tanks, an updated cockpit configuration, and upgraded avionics for both offensive and defensive operations.

The Kfir can be employed in the strike, ground-attack, and air-superiority roles. As an air-superiority fighter, the Kfir is armed with an assortment of air-to-air missiles. In the ground-attack role, it may be fitted with up to 12,730 pounds of ordnance on nine hard points—five on the fuselage and two on each wing. The Kfir is also armed with two 30 millimeter cannons.

Missile-armed Israeli Kfir fighters in low-altitude flight. The Kfir is also armed with two powerful 30mm multibarrel cannons.

While the Israeli Air Force now uses its F-15s and F-16s as first-line fighters, the scrappy Kfir is used for both ground-attack and electronic warfare.

ISRAEL AIRCRAFT INDUSTRIES KFIR-C7

Wingspan:	26 ft., 11.5 in.
Length:	51 ft., 4.25 in.
Height:	14 ft., 11.25 in.
Weight (maximum take-off):	36,376 lbs.
Engine:	One General Electric J79-J1E turbojet
Engine thrust:	18,750 lbs.
Maximum speed:	1,516 mph
Maximum range:	2,008 miles
Service ceiling:	58,000 ft.

MiG-21MF Fishbed

Mikoyan-Gurevich MiG-21MF Fishbed—Iraq

A veteran of the Vietnam War, the MiG-21 is used by Iraq as a short-range, highly maneuverable interceptor.

Small, maneuverable, and heavily armed, the MiG-21 Fishbed, seen here with Soviet markings, is suitable as both an air-superiority fighter and a ground-attack plane.

The MiG-21, NATO codenamed Fishbed, has been widely used in the Soviet Air Force and exported to more than 34 nations, including Iraq. Iraq also uses a MiG-21 variant manufactured in the Peoples Republic of China, where it is designated the J-7. Iraq has approximately 150 MiG-21s and another 40 of the J-7 variant.

Originally designed as a low-altitude air-superiority fighter, later versions of the MiG-21 added a light strike capability. The first production model, the MiG-21F, entered service with the Soviet Air Force in 1959 as a clear-weather, day-only fighter interceptor.

No-frills fighter

In essence, the MiG-21 is a no-frills, highly maneuverable air-superiority fighter than can be adapted for the ground-attack role. It is quite small, and its combat radius is limited by its small internal fuel capacity. Hard points on the wings carry a range of air-to-air missiles; air-to-ground missiles and bombs are used in a light strike role. The MiG-21 was originally designed to carry two 30 millimeter NR-30 cannons, but the left gun had to be removed to meet weight restrictions and to provide room for avionics.

The model seen most often in non-Soviet air forces is the MiG-21bis. This version is far more powerful than the original MiG-21, and it carries a heavier weight of armament. A refinement of this version, NATO codenamed Fishbed-N, carries improved avionics and mounts two radar-homing AA-2C Atoll and two AA-8 Aphid air-to-air missiles.

MIG-21MF FISHBED-J

Wingspan:	23 ft., 5.5 in.
Length:	51 ft., 8.5 in.
Height:	13 ft., 5.5 in.
Weight (maximum take-off):	20,725 lbs.
Engine:	One Tumansky R-13-300 turbojet
Engine thrust:	14,550 lbs.
Maximum speed:	Mach 2.1
Maximum range:	1,118 miles
Service ceiling:	50,000 ft.

MiG-23 Flogger
Mikoyan-Gurevich MiG-23 Flogger—Iraq

The MiG-23, NATO codenamed Flogger, was designed in the early 1960s as an air-superiority fighter for frontal aviation units. It was assigned the roles of fighter, fighter interceptor, and ground-attack.

The MiG-23 was the first Soviet fighter equipped with variable-sweep wings. All versions of the MiG-23 can be armed with the 23 millimeter GSh-23 twin-barrel cannon carried beneath the fuselage. Various hard points under the fuselage, air intake ducts, and the fixed wing panels can carry a range of bombs, rocket packs, and air-to-air missiles. In Soviet service, the air intake hard points can mount twin launchers for four AA-8 (Aphid) close-range missiles. Medium-range missiles (AA-7 Apex) can be carried on the wing pylons.

Originally, the MiG-23 was intended to serve as an air combat fighter. Continuous improvements have produced a very versatile aircraft. The MiG-23BN is an export version of the ground-attack model. It is armed with the AS-7 air-to-surface missile and the 23mm GSh-23 cannon. A second version of the BN model has a radar warning system installed on each side of the aircraft just ahead of the nosewheel doors.

Warsaw Pact mainstay

The MiG-23 remains the most numerous Soviet fighter in the tactical air-defense and home air-defense units. All former Warsaw Pact air forces are equipped with MiG-23s, as are the air forces of 12 other nations including, most particularly, Iraq.

MiG-23 Flogger comes in for a landing.

Probably built in greater numbers than any other fighter of its time, the MiG-23 is the most important Iraqi ground-attack plane.

MIG-23MF FLOGGER

Wingspan (unswept):	46 ft., 9 in.
Wingspan (swept):	26 ft., 9.5 in.
Length:	59 ft., 6.5 in.
Height:	14 ft., 9 in.
Weight (maximum take-off):	41,670 lbs.
Engine:	One Tumansky 29B turbojet
Engine thrust:	27,500 lbs.
Maximum speed:	Mach 2.35
Maximum range:	Unavailable
Combat radius:	715 miles
Service ceiling:	61,000 ft.

MiG-29 Fulcrum

Mikoyan-Gurevich MiG-29 Fulcrum—Iraq

The MiG-29, NATO codenamed Fulcrum, is perhaps the Soviet Union's most capable fighter interceptor and most agile aircraft. It was originally designed as an air-superiority fighter, but after further development, the ground-attack role was added. The aircraft first flew in the early 1980s and was operational with Soviet air forces by 1985.

The MiG-29 is a single-seat aircraft, although the Fulcrum B variant has two seats for the training role. In the fighter role, the MiG-29 is armed with one 30 millimeter multibarrel cannon in the left wing. On three pylons under each wing it also carries AA-10 air-to-air missiles for long-range and AA-11 missiles for short-range work. In the attack mode, the aircraft can also carry the three sizes of air-to-ground rockets used by Soviet forces: 240mm, 80mm, and 57mm, as well as a variety of gravity bombs.

Sophisticated

The MiG-29 Fulcrum has a pulse-doppler look-down/shoot-down radar that can identify enemy aircraft flying below it and then direct air-to-air missiles against the enemy aircraft. It is thought that this radar is not able to track an enemy aircraft while searching for additional threats.

The MiG-29 is certain to remain in frontline service with the Soviet Union well into the next century. In addition to Iraq, Fulcrums are also flown by the air forces of various nations allied with the Soviet Union.

The MiG-29 has dazzled American crowds at air-shows and impressed the American pilots lucky enough to fly it. The Iraqis entered the war with about 30 of these world-class planes.

The most advanced fighter in Iraq's Air Force is the Soviet-built MiG-29 Fulcrum.

MiG-29 FULCRUM-A

Wingspan:	37 ft., 8.75 in.
Length:	56 ft., 8 in.
Height:	14 ft., 5.25 in.
Weight (maximum take-off):	39,000 lbs.
Engines:	Two Tumansky RD-33 turbofans
Engine thrust:	18,300 lbs.
Maximum speed:	Mach 2.3
Maximum range:	1,300 miles
Service ceiling:	56,000 ft.

A-6 Intruder

Grumman A-6 Intruder—United States

The A-6 Intruder is a versatile two-seat, medium-attack aircraft with all-weather, day-night attack capabilities. All A-6 variants feature a side-by-side seating arrangement typical of much larger planes. The pilot occupies the left seat, while the weapons system operator/navigator occupies the seat on the right.

Laser-guided

The first A-6 variant was flown in 1960. The most numerous variant is the A-6E, which was introduced in 1970. All A-6Es have since been converted into the A-6E/TRAM (Target Recognition and Attack Multisensor). TRAM's electronics, which are carried in a turret located under the nose, include infrared- and laser-targeting sensors and multimode radar. The lasers are used in conjunction with laser-guided weapons. The TRAM system on an A-6E can illuminate a target with a laser while a second A-6E launches weapons against it, using the first A-6E's laser reflection to guide the projectile.

The A-6E may also be armed with nuclear bombs, conventional "iron" bombs, and AGM-84 Harpoon antiship missiles. The maximum combined load of ordnance and drop tanks is 18,000 pounds.

The EA-6B Prowler is an electronic warfare Intruder variant with a crew of four. In order to accommodate the additional two crew members (who operate electronic-countermeasures hardware), the Prowler is five feet longer than the Intruder. Each Prowler is equipped to carry two AGM-88A High-speed Antiradiation Missiles (HARM), which home in on enemy radar transmitters.

An A-6 Intruder prepares to take off from an aircraft carrier.

An old soldier from the Vietnam War, the venerable, versatile A-6E Intruder can carry up to 18,000 pounds of external stores.

GRUMMAN A-6E INTRUDER

Wingspan:	53 ft.
Length:	54 ft., 9 in.
Height:	16 ft., 2 in.
Weight (maximum take-off):	60,400 lbs.
Engines:	Two Pratt & Whitney J52-P-8B turbojets
Engine thrust:	9,300 lbs.
Maximum speed (sea level):	648 mph
Maximum range:	2,740 miles
Service ceiling:	42,400 ft.

AV-8B Harrier II

McDonnell Douglas AV-8B Harrier II—United States

The AV-8B Harrier II is an outgrowth of a design pioneered by the Hawker aircraft company in Britain. After its British debut in the late 1960s, this vertical take-off and landing (VTOL) aircraft attracted the attention of the U.S. Marine Corps, which was interested in using Harriers for close air support of amphibious operations. The Marines subsequently ordered 110 Harriers, which entered service in 1971 as the AV-8A Harrier.

In 1975, McDonnell Douglas developed an improved Harrier with a larger wing that nearly doubled the aircraft's range and payload. By 1982, a joint manufacturing agreement had been worked out between British Aerospace (which had absorbed Hawker) and McDonnell Douglas whereby the American company would produce the up-rated VTOL aircraft as the AV-8B Harrier II. The Marine Corps AV-8B can be armed with a 25 millimeter cannon, a four-ton bomb load, or a variety of guided air-to-ground munitions, as well as the AIM-9L Sidewinder air-to-air missile.

To support a Desert Storm ground war, vertical take-off Harriers work close behind the lines, making sortie after sortie, using digital maps generated on-site.

The AV-8B Harrier II is unique among fixed wing aircraft in its ability to take off and land vertically.

Falkland ace

When Argentina invaded the British-owned Falkland Islands in the south Atlantic, Royal Navy Harriers flew more than 2,000 attack missions and in the fighter role shot down at least 20 enemy aircraft without a single loss. Today's U.S. Marine Corps AV-8B Harriers would fly and fight in much the same way the British Harriers did in the Falklands: in support of a joint Navy/Marines amphibious assault landing or in the context of Marine operations ashore.

McDONNELL DOUGLAS AV-8B HARRIER II

Wingspan:	30 ft., 4 in.
Length:	46 ft., 4 in.
Height:	11 ft., 7.75 in.
Weight (maximum take-off):	29,750 lbs.
Engine:	One Rolls-Royce F402-RR-402 turbojet
Engine thrust:	21,500 lbs.
Maximum speed:	683 mph
Maximum range:	2,015 miles
Service ceiling:	50,000 ft.

A-10 Thunderbolt II

Fairchild Republic A-10 Thunderbolt II—United States

Nobody calls the A-10 the Thunderbolt. Even its most ardent proponents call it the Warthog. Ugly and misshapen though it may be, it is nonetheless the deadliest ground-attack aircraft in any nation's air force.

Tank buster

The first A-10 variant was flown in 1972 and entered Air Force service shortly thereafter as the A-10A. The single-seat A-10 is especially effective as a "tank-busting" aircraft. Its main armament is a formidable GAU-8 Avenger 30 millimeter rotary cannon with 1,200 rounds. This seven-barrel weapon fires high-velocity slugs with depleted uranium tips. Depleted uranium, which is not radioactive, is heavier than lead or steel and thus has penetrating power against heavy tank armor.

In addition to the Avenger, the A-10 can carry eight tons of air-to-ground munitions, including "iron" bombs, "smart" bombs, cluster bombs, AGM-65 air-to-ground Maverick missiles, and AIM-9 Sidewinder air-to-air missiles. Electronic counter-measures equipment can also be carried on the A-10's eight underwing pylons.

The Warthog is one of the "hardest" aircraft flying. The pilot sits in a titanium-armor "bathtub" that can withstand incoming rounds from 23mm cannons. Control lines are duplicated and stretched through widely separate parts of the aircraft. The heavily armored engines are located high and to the rear of the fuselage for maximum shielding from ground-launched heat-seeking missiles.

Although the A-10 Thunderbolt II is a tank killer, a pair of them were involved in a dramatic rescue of a downed American pilot behind enemy lines.

The A-10 "Warthog" is admired by its pilots and feared by enemies on the ground. It proved unexpectedly versatile when used against heavily defended ground targets.

FAIRCHILD REPUBLIC A-10A THUNDERBOLT II

Wingspan:	57 ft., 6 in.
Length:	53 ft., 4 in.
Height:	14 ft., 8 in.
Weight (maximum take-off):	50,000 lbs.
Engines:	Two General Electric TF34-GE-100 turbofans
Engine thrust:	9,065 lbs.
Maximum speed:	439 mph
Maximum range:	2,454 miles
Service ceiling:	30,500 ft.

F-117A Stealth
Lockheed F-117A Stealth Fighter—United States

The F-117A Nighthawk Stealth Fighter was one of the first aircraft to see action in Operation Desert Storm.

In the first wave of the American Desert Storm attack, F-117As showed incredible accuracy in weapons delivery.

The F-117A Stealth fighter was actually in service for six years before the Air Force even admitted its existence. This super-secret aircraft was born in 1978 at Lockheed's so-called "Skunk Works" in Burbank, California, which has developed so many other advanced aircraft for the Air Force.

The F-117A was designed to be as invisible to radar as possible, as well as difficult to see visually. Its shape is somewhat like a large, flat delta—or perhaps an arrowhead.

Invisible to radar

The F-117A is a single-seat, twin-engine aircraft. The cockpit is set low in the front of the fuselage. The engines, buried in the wing roots and deeply recessed to minimize their infrared signature, are located above the fuselage centerline. The skin covering is composed of panels of small, flat surfaces that reflect radar signals in every direction. Almost all of the external surface is coated with radar-absorbent material.

The F-117A is equipped with fly-by-wire controls, which suggests that the aircraft is unstable in flight and needs the constant attention of the flight control computer to keep it flying. The fly-by-wire controls would account for observers' reports of the aircraft's extraordinary maneuverability and the nickname bestowed by its pilots: the "Wobbly Goblin."

The Air Force first flew the F-117A in 1981, and from 1981 to 1989 the F-117A was flown only at night to maintain secrecy. The primary mission of the aircraft probably entails low-level precision attack on high-priority targets with smart bombs or air-to-surface missiles stowed in internal bays. The F-117A received its baptism of combat in December 1989, when two F-117As flew from Nellis Air Force Base to Panama. The aircraft dropped several 2,000-pound bombs with pinpoint accuracy on the headquarters of the Panamanian Defense Forces 6th and 7th Infantry Division at Rio Hato.

LOCKHEED F-117A STEALTH FIGHTER

Wingspan:	43 ft., 4 in.
Length:	65 ft., 11 in.
Height:	12 ft., 5 in.
Weight (maximum take-off):	52,500 lbs.
Engines:	Two General Electric F404-GE-F1D2 turbofans
Engine thrust:	11,000 lbs.
Maximum speed:	Mach 0.9
Maximum range:	1,250 miles
Service ceiling:	52,500 ft.

GR.Mk1 Jaguar

SEPECAT Jaguar GR.Mk1—Britain

The Jaguar GR.Mk1 primarily serves as a supersonic attack fighter with the air forces of Great Britain and France. In 1987 French Jaguars sent to support the government of Chad attacked and drove off Libyan infantry and armored units allied with Chadian anti-government forces.

Joint venture

The Jaguar was the result of a British-French joint development project started in 1965 and completed in 1973. Two companies—British Aerospace in Great Britain and Bregeut in France—were selected to develop and build the aircraft; they formed a joint venture known as SEPECAT. The first prototype flew on September 8, 1968.

Between 1973 and 1982, the Royal Air Force received 165 single-seat Jaguars configured for the attack role. The French Air Force acquired 160 single-seat Jaguar variants. All Jaguars were equipped with an engine jointly designed and built by Rolls-Royce of Great Britain and Turbomecca of France.

The Jaguar can carry a mix of cannons and "smart" and gravity bombs. French Jaguars are equipped with either two DEFA 553 or two Aden 30 millimeter fuselage-mounted guns. A fuselage pylon and four wing pylons can carry up to 10,000 pounds of armament, ranging from nuclear bombs to air-to-ground missiles to rocket pods. The pylons also carry fuel tanks, electronic emission detectors, and jamming pods. Along with Britain and France, Italy is fielding a Jaguar-equipped squadron in the Desert Storm offensive.

The Jaguar is a strike-fighter aircraft able to carry a mix of cannons and smart and gravity bombs.

The Jaguar has been flown in combat by French, British, Saudi, and Italian air forces. It can operate from extremely rough desert fields with a full load.

SEPECAT JAGUAR GR.MK1

Wingspan:	28 ft., 6 in.
Length:	55 ft., 2.5 in.
Height:	15 ft., 9.5 in
Weight (maximum take-off):	34,612 lbs.
Engines:	Two Rolls-Royce Adour Mk 102 turbofans
Engine thrust:	7,306 lbs.
Maximum speed (sea level):	Mach 1.1
Maximum range:	1,902 miles
Service ceiling:	45,000 ft.

Tornado
Panavia Tornado—Britain and Italy

Great Britain's most capable attack plane—the Tornado IDS—can also perform many other roles, from interception to reconnaissance.

Bolkow-Blohm, and Aeritalia. The purpose of this consortium was to design and build a new attack aircraft according to recently established NATO criteria.

Panavia subsequently produced the Tornado Interdictor/Strike (IDS) model and the Tornado Air-Defense Variant (ADV). The Tornado made its first flight in August 1974, and initial orders were placed almost immediately by all the countries involved in the project.

Long-distance cruiser
The Tornado is a two-seat aircraft with variable-geometry wings. With the wings swept forward (25 degrees), the aircraft can take off and land at forward airfields not accessible to other fixed wing aircraft; it can also loiter over a specific area or cruise for long distances. With the wings swept back (66 degrees), the Tornado can move quickly to attack advancing enemy aircraft as well as perform close air support missions at high speeds and low altitudes.

Both IDS and ADV versions are night and all-weather capable. The IDV is armed with two 27 millimeter guns and up to 19,840 pounds of ordnance (including various missiles, bombs, rocket pods, and electronic countermeasures systems), which are carried on seven fuselage and wing hard points. The Tornado ADV, which is used only by the Royal Air Force, is armed with air-to-air missiles and a 27mm multibarrel cannon. In addition to the British and Italian air forces, Tornados are flown by the Saudi Arabian air force.

In 1969, Britain, West Germany, and Italy formed Panavia, a consortium comprising the three largest aircraft manufacturers in Western Europe: British Aerospace, Messerschmitt-

PANAVIA TORNADO IDS

Wingspan (unswept):	45 ft., 7 in.
Wingspan (swept):	28 ft., 2 in.
Length:	54 ft., 10 in.
Height:	19 ft., 6.75 in.
Weight (maximum take-off):	60,000 lbs.
Engines:	Two Turbo-Union RB-199 Mk 103 turbofans
Engine thrust:	16,920 lbs.
Maximum speed:	Mach 2.2
Maximum range:	1,525 miles
Service ceiling:	70,000 ft.

Su-17/20/22 Fitter

Sukhoi Su-17/20/22 Fitter—Iraq

No other Soviet aircraft causes as much confusion regarding designations as the Sukhoi Su-17/20/22 attack bomber series does. The designations Su-20 and Su-22 are for export variations only. NATO has codenamed all variations in Soviet service as Su-17 Fitter, followed by a letter suffix.

Experimental origins

The Su-17 began its career in the early 1960s as an experimental Su-7 Fitter that had been rebuilt to test a variable-geometry wing concept. The Su-17 Fitter-C (operational since 1971) is the basic version of this series. It was built in relatively small numbers and also serves with the Soviet Navy. Among other countries, a version with reduced electronics capacity has been exported to Iraq.

It is armed with two NR-30 30 millimeter cannons mounted in the wing roots. Additionally, either six or eight hard points carry air-to-ground missiles, and/or four 298-gallon external fuel tanks. Some Su-17s are also configured to carry the AA-2 Atoll air-to-air missile.

The Soviets refer to the Su-17 Fitter-D as the Su-17M. It is quite similar to the Fitter-C, but the forward fuselage has been lengthened to make room for increased electronics capability. A pod housing terrain-avoidance radar was added under the nose, and a laser range finder has been fitted into the air intake center cone. The export version of this model is called the Su-22, or the Fitter-F.

This is a Soviet Su-17 Fitter; Iraq flies the export version of this plane—the Su-20.

A partial "swing-wing" aircraft—the wing pivots farther outboard than in most designs—the Fitter is a tough ground-attack aircraft.

Su-20 FITTER-C

Wingspan (unswept):	45 ft., 11.5 in
Wingspan (swept):	32 ft., 6 in.
Length:	61 ft., 6.25 in.
Height:	15 ft., 7 in.
Weight (maximum take-off):	39,020 lbs.
Engine:	One Lyulka AL-21-F turbojet
Engine thrust:	24,700 lbs.
Maximum speed:	Mach 2.17
Maximum range:	Unavailable
Combat radius:	425 miles
Service ceiling:	59,050 ft.

B-52 Stratofortress

Boeing B-52 Stratofortress—United States

The venerable B-52 was involved in Desert Storm from the first night, doing what it does best, dropping tens of thousands of iron bombs.

Starting in the early stages of Operation Desert Storm, B-52 Stratofortresses have been bombing Iraq's elite Republican Brigade.

The Boeing B-52 Stratofortress has survived in front-line service for *three* generations. There are crew members flying aboard B-52s whose grandfathers flew B-52s.

Development of the plane that would become the B-52 began in the late 1940s, when the Air Force saw a need for an all-jet bomber that could carry nuclear and conventional bombs more than 4,000 miles. The B-52 made its first flight in 1952 and entered service with the U.S. Air Force's Strategic Air Command (SAC) in 1954.

In 1965, SAC B-52s began conducting Operation Arc Light carpet-bombing raids on suspected Viet Cong strongholds in South Vietnam. In 1972, SAC B-52s based in Guam and Thailand conducted an 11-day series of strategic bombing missions against Hanoi, an action that paved the way for a cease-fire in the war.

"Big Ugly Fat Fellow"

Known as the Big Ugly Fat Fellow (BUFF), the B-52 can carry up to 60,000 pounds of bombs, or a mixture of bombs and cruise missiles in internal bays and on underwing pylons. A remote control tail turret is armed with either four .50 caliber machine guns or a 20 millimeter multibarrel cannon. Advanced electronic systems and terrain-avoidance radar allow for low-level, long-range penetration missions under virtually any conditions.

The variants presently in U.S. Air Force service are the B-52G and B-52H. There is every indication that the B-52H will serve until the mid-1990s, or even beyond. As in Vietnam, in Operation Desert Storm B-52s were used to carpet-bomb Iraqi troop concentrations. Its success there proved that there is no substitute for load-carrying capability.

BOEING B-52H STRATOFORTRESS

Wingspan:	185 ft.
Length:	160 ft., 11 in.
Height:	40 ft., 8 in.
Weight (maximum take-off):	488,000 lbs.
Engines:	Eight Pratt & Whitney TF33-P-3 turbofans
Engine thrust:	13,750 lbs.
Maximum speed:	595 mph
Maximum range:	10,145 miles
Service ceiling:	55,000 ft.

F-111/FB-111 Aardvark

General Dynamics F-111/FB-111 Aardvark—United States

The F-111 first flew in 1964 under the TFX (tactical fighter, experimental) designation. Entering Air Force service in 1967, it saw action in the Vietnam War, where structural defects and problems with the terrain-following radar caused the loss of several aircraft. Withdrawn for modifications, the F-111 was reintroduced with considerable success in 1972, earning the nickname Whispering Death from the Viet Cong.

Long-range, deep-interdiction

Dubbed Aardvark, the F-111 is now favored by Tactical Air Command (TAC) units for use on long-range, deep-interdiction attacks against targets within enemy territory. The F-111B is used by the Strategic Air Command as a medium bomber.

The Aardvark has side-by-side seating for the pilot and weapons systems operator, and can fly at Mach 2 speed while carrying 12 tons of bombs and missiles. The FB-111 can carry a 16-ton nuclear or conventional bomb load, or 13 tons of bombs and four AGM-69 Short-range Attack Missiles carried on swiveling pylons located beneath the variable-geometry wings. A Pave Track laser designator system enables pinpoint delivery of ordnance. The F-111's wings can be changed in flight from a straight to swept-back delta configuration.

On April 15, 1986, 18 Aardvarks supported by U.S. Air Force refueling planes conducted punitive strikes against Libya, which had sponsored terrorist attacks against U.S. military personnel in Europe.

The F-111 Aardvark has seen action in the Mideast before; 'Varks bombed Libya in 1986.

About 70 F-111s were designated for use in the war against Iraq.

GENERAL DYNAMICS F-111F AARDVARK

Wingspan (unswept):	63 ft.
Wingspan (swept):	32 ft.
Length:	73 ft., 6 in.
Height:	17 ft.
Weight (maximum take-off):	100,000 + lbs.
Engines:	Two Pratt & Whitney JF30-P-100 turbofans
Engine thrust:	25,100 lbs.
Maximum speed:	Mach 2.5
Maximum range:	3,378 miles
Service ceiling:	60,000 + ft.

E-3 Sentry
Boeing E-3 Sentry (AWACS)—United States

Boeing Model 707, which was designed to be configured with state-of-the-art electronics inside and topped with a 30-foot rotating radome. The aircraft are designated AWACS; the acronym stands for Airborne Warning and Control System.

The first of two dozen E-3A Sentrys were delivered in 1977, and all 24 went into service on January 1, 1979. Although flown by the Air Force Tactical Air Command (TAC), they first saw duty with the joint U.S./Canadian North American Air Defense Command (NORAD).

New and improved

An improvement program begun in 1984 has seen the A model superseded by the E-3B and the E-3C. The improvements have included a larger number of situation display consoles (SDC), a better Have Quick radar jamming system, and an upgraded Joint Tactical Information Distribution System (JTIDS) and Tactical Digital Information Link (TADIL).

As the world discovered when an Iranian airliner was shot down by mistake in the Persian Gulf in 1988, battlefield electronics are only as good as the people who operate them. Decisions are only as good as the precision of the information upon which they are based. This makes IFF (Identification, Friend or Foe) recognition a vital part of the AWACS task. In Operation Desert Storm, these planes form an interlocking, yet noninterfering, network of command posts able to manage the hundreds of warplanes that might be airborne at any given moment.

If there was ever an "indispensable" weapon, it is the E-3 AWACS, which is capable of directing UN forces with tremendous accuracy. The big plane acts as the brain of the electronic warfare central nervous system.

The command and control abilities of the E-3 Sentry AWACS make possible the thousands of sorties flown against Iraq.

The E-3 Sentry is the most sophisticated airborne command post ever devised. The airframe chosen for the job was the

BOEING E-3 SENTRY (AWACS)

Wingspan:	145 ft., 9 in.
Length:	152 ft., 11 in.
Height:	41 ft., 9 in.
Weight (maximum take-off):	325,000 lbs.
Engines:	Four Pratt & Whitney TF33-PW-100/100A turbofans
Engine thrust:	21,000 lbs.
Maximum speed:	530 mph
Maximum range:	7,475 miles
Service ceiling:	29,000 ft.

F-4G Wild Weasel

McDonnell Douglas F-4G Wild Weasel—United States

Like a wonderful old fire horse, the McDonnell Douglas F-4G Phantom is back in action, this time in the absolutely vital role of "Wild Weasel," suppressing Iraqi radars and missile sites.

Indomitable warhorse

The F-4 is without question the most important single fighter to emerge in the free world in the last two decades. Originally submitted by McDonnell as a speculative bid, the F-4 became the mainstay of three services—the Air Force, the Navy, and the Marines. In addition to use by 11 foreign countries, it is still in front-line American service 32 years after its first flight. (To put this in perspective, similar longevity for the World War I Spad would have permitted it to fly in the Korean War.)

The first Wild Weasels came into being to suppress the Soviet-built SA-2 SAMs and "Fan Song" radars that the North Vietnamese were using in 1965. North American F-100 Sabres were used first, but as the program developed, both Republic F-105 and McDonnell Douglas F-4 aircraft were successfully pressed into service.

The F-4G Wild Weasel seeks out radar emitters and then launches AGM-88 HARM or AGM-45A Shrike missiles. The High-speed Antiradiation Missile (HARM) is the key to the incredible success in Iraq of the F-4G Weasel crews. The HARM has an excellent stand-off capability combined with fantastic accuracy and devastating power. HARMs can work even if they aren't fired, for enemy radars will often just shut down rather than run the risk of destruction; when this happens,

the attacking "force package" can get in almost undetected.

The F-4G's are aging, however, and getting adequate spare parts is one of the most difficult tasks that Air Force crew chiefs have to cope with.

Wild Weasels—modified F-4 Phantoms—run high-risk missions to expose and disable enemy radar positions.

MCDONNELL DOUGLAS F4-G "WILD WEASEL" PHANTOM II

Wingspan:	38 ft., 5 in.
Length:	63 ft.
Height:	16 ft., 3 in.
Weight (maximum take-off):	60,630 lbs.
Engines:	Two General Electric J79-15 turbojets
Engine thrust:	17,900 lbs.
Maximum speed:	1,464 mph
Maximum range:	2,300 miles
Service ceiling:	59,200 ft.

AH-64A Apache

McDonnell Douglas AH-64A Apache—United States

The lethal-looking, heavily armed and armored AH-64A Apache plays for the Army the same role the A-10 Warthog plays for the Air Force: tank killer.

An integral part of any ground attack is the AH-64 Apache attack helicopter.

The AH-64A Apache is specifically designed for the attack role. The first production model was rolled out on September 30, 1983, and the first delivery to the Army was made on January 26 of the following year.

The Apache is armed with a McDonnell Douglas M230 30 millimeter multibarrel gun and up to 16 laser-guided Hellfire antitank missiles. The Hellfires have a range of more than 3.7 miles and can penetrate the armor of any known main battle tank. The Apache may also be armed with 2.75-inch folding-fin aerial rockets. All rockets are carried on two stub wings that provide additional lift and may serve as attaching points for external fuel tanks.

Hard to kill

The Apache was designed to be crashworthy. Armor made of boron carbide bonded to Kevlar protects the Apache crew and the helicopter's vital systems. Blast shields, which protect against 23mm or smaller high-explosive incendiary ammunition, separate the pilot and copilot/weapons operator from each other; thus, both crew members cannot be incapacitated by a single round. Armored seats and airframe armor can withstand rounds up to .50 caliber of armor-piercing incendiary shot.

The Apache's main rotor has four blades composed of stainless steel spars and glass fiber tubes. They can cut through tree branches up to two inches in diameter or withstand .50 caliber machine gun or 23mm high-explosive shell strikes. Fuel cells, located forward and aft of the ammunition bay, are self-sealing against .50 caliber rounds and can absorb the impact of rounds up to 23mm.

McDONNELL DOUGLAS AH-64A APACHE

Main rotor diameter:	48 ft.
Tail rotor diameter:	9 ft., 2 in.
Length:	48 ft., 2 in.
Height:	12 ft., 7 in.
Weight (maximum take-off):	21,000 lbs.
Maximum speed:	184 mph
Maximum range:	300 miles
Service ceiling:	21,000 ft.

AH-1S HueyCobra

AH-1S HueyCobra (Bell Model 209)—United States

In 1965, Bell Helicopter introduced a specific Huey variation to serve as an armed escort helicopter for transport and medevac choppers. The initial model designation of the HueyCobra was AH-1G. Distinguishing features included a new, thin-profile fuselage and stub wings designed to ease the load on the main rotor and serve as attaching points for additional weapons. The narrow fuselage dictated a tandem cockpit seating arrangement, with the pilot placed behind and above the copilot/weapons operator.

Fly 'n' fire

A turret was mounted under the nose of the fuselage to carry miniguns, rapid-firing cannons, or grenade launchers. The weapons are controlled by the copilot/weapons operator. When the copilot/weapons operator releases the weapon controls, the turret resumes a locked fore and aft position and the pilot can fire the weapons while flying the helicopter. Aiming in this case is done by turning the helicopter. The copilot/weapons operator can also fly the helicopter.

The first HueyCobra model to be armed with the B6M-71 TOW antitank missile was the AH-1Q, which was intended as an interim solution until the modernized HueyCobra, the AH-1S, could be developed. The first AH-1S entered Army service in March 1977. Subsequent AH-1S variants were equipped with a universal turret mounting either a 20 millimeter or 30mm gun. Other versions of the HueyCobra include the United States Marines' AH-1T SeaCobra.

Ground forces operating in the Mideast receive strong combat support from AH-1S HueyCobras.

Like its predecessors in the Vietnam War, the HueyCobra offers potent firepower for use against Iraqi tank forces.

BELL AH-1S HUEYCOBRA

Main rotor diameter:	44 ft.
Tail rotor diameter:	8 ft., 6 in.
Length:	44 ft., 7 in.
Height:	13 ft., 5 in.
Weight (maximum take-off):	10,000 lbs.
Maximum speed:	141 mph
Maximum range:	315 miles
Service ceiling:	12,200 ft.

OH-58C Scout

OH-58C Scout—United States

In the sandy environment of Desert Storm, the versatility and ease of repair of the OH-58C Scout has proved invaluable.

No helicopter likes desert sand, but the OH-58C Scout—versatile and easy to repair—has shown itself to good advantage in the Desert Storm campaign.

The growth of the Bell OH-58 aircraft from an experimental prototype in 1962 to a versatile, gunslinging instrument of war today speaks well for both the original design and for the more than 40 air forces using the basic Model 206 design. In this process, the designers have been able to extract the aircraft's full performance potential.

Good breeding

Few helicopters have had so illustrious a pedigree as the OH-58C, from the very first two-seaters put out by Bell to the magnificent series of Hueys that became a combat stalwart in Vietnam. And even fewer helicopters have sired such a distinguished line of follow-on aircraft, the Jet Ranger series.

The Scout is, of course, much smaller than the Huey, with its maximum loaded weight of 3,200 pounds being approximately one-third that of its predecessor's. Yet so versatile is the basic design that it has been stretched to the OH-58D configuration, with a four-bladed rotor and a 4,500-pound gross weight.

The OH-58C typifies Bell design and construction, featuring the patented Bell semi-rigid main rotor, and using the 420 shaft horsepower Allison Model 250 turboshaft engine.

Standard armament for the OH-58C is the Army's M26 armament sub-system, but special requirements by other buyers have created a vast array of possibilities. Among the options are depth bombs, rocket launchers, searchlights, Hellfire missiles, TOW launchers, cable cutters, smoke and flare dispensers, multi-task machine gun pods, and twin Stinger launchers.

In Iraq, the conditions of desert warfare are especially cruel to helicopters, with sand abrading rotors, entering gearboxes, ruining engines, and causing equipment to malfunction. The long experience that Bell service engineers have with their product, and their ability to obtain quick fixes to field problems goes a long way to offset these difficulties.

BELL OH-58C SCOUT

Main rotor diameter:	35 ft., 4 in.
Length:	41 ft.
Height:	9 ft., 6.5 in.
Weight (maximum take-off):	3,200 lbs.
Cruising speed:	120 mph
Maximum range:	300 miles

Harpoon

Harpoon Antiship Missile—United States

Until the 1950s, the major aerial threat to ships came from aircraft that would dive in and unload a free-fall gravity bomb. The bomb was designed to either explode on impact or bury itself deep within the ship before detonating. Today, long-range attack aircraft, as well as ships, can launch devastatingly accurate explosive missiles equipped with conventional or nuclear warheads. The Harpoon is one of the most deadly surface-to-surface antiship missiles in the U.S. Navy's inventory and has been developed into the highly effective SLAM for airborne use.

Flexibility is the key

The Harpoon began its life in 1968 as an air-to-surface missile and quickly showed an improbable flexibility. Today, the Harpoon is a short- to medium-range, all-weather, antiship missile that can be launched from aircraft, and from ships and submarines as well. It carries a high-explosive fragmentation warhead. The missile skims over the sea waves at a speed of Mach .75 to a range of more than 69 miles to find its target. In a standard launch, the Harpoon follows a ballistic path during its boost phase and then descends to a sea-skimming flight altitude controlled by the inertial autopilot and radar altimeter. When the missile nears the target, the active radar activates, searches for and acquires the target. Once acquired, the radar guides the missile to the target.

In the past, the Harpoon performed a "terminal maneuver"; the missile would suddenly fly upward, or "pop-up," and then dive on the target.

The Harpoon missile is so versatile that it can be launched from ships as well as submarines and aircraft.

This maneuver has been discontinued because more sophisticated ship-borne anti-missile systems made the Harpoon too vulnerable.

A remarkably versatile weapon, the Harpoon missile is mounted on numerous vessels in the Gulf, often in concert with the Tomahawk missile. Whatever its target, an approaching Harpoon is not a welcome sight.

HARPOON ANTISHIP MISSILE

Length:	15 ft., 1 in.
Diameter:	1 ft., 1 in.
Weight:	1,498 lbs.
Speed:	600 mph
Range:	92 miles
Warhead:	488-lb. high-explosive

Sidewinder and Maverick

Sidewinder and Maverick Missiles—United States

Still tough after all these years: That describes the veteran Sidewinder and Maverick missiles, which have taken a heavy toll on Iraqi targets.

Ground crew members load a Maverick missile before a sortie.

The Sidewinder is an effective air-to-air missile.

While some notable new weapons have been introduced into service in the war with Iraq, the U.S. military and many of its allies continue to rely on a number of missiles of demonstrated reliability and performance. Two of these are the heat-seeking Sidewinder and the optically guided Maverick.

Old but effective

In terms of years of operation, the AIM-9 Sidewinder may be considered an elderly weapon. However, almost continuous upgrading has kept it at the forefront of guided missiles used around the world. A heat-seeker, the Sidewinder is now far more capable of maneuver than it was during its Vietnam days.

Unlike many of its contemporaries, the Sidewinder is considered by the Air Force to still have room for further development. The Air Force will probably be using the missile well into the next century.

Another old standby is the AGM-65 Maverick missile, which has an automatic homing capability that enables the pilot to acquire a target, fire the round, and have the 464-pound Maverick automatically track into the target.

The Maverick has gained worldwide acceptance, and is used by 18 Allied nations. The latest U.S. versions have a refinement badly needed in Iraq: the ability to determine by infra-red radiation detection whether its target is a "live" tank or just a hulk.

SIDEWINDER AND MAVERICK MISSILES

Length:	
Sidewinder:	9 ft., 5 in.
Maverick:	8 ft., 2 in.
Weight:	
Sidewinder:	191 lbs. at launch
Maverick:	462 lbs. at launch
Guidance:	
Sidewinder:	Infrared
Maverick:	Electro-optical
Warhead:	
Sidewinder:	20.8 lbs.
Maverick:	83 lbs.
Range:	
Sidewinder:	10 miles
Maverick:	14 miles

F-14 Tomcat ▲   F-15 Eagle ▼

The Persian Gulf: a region in crisis

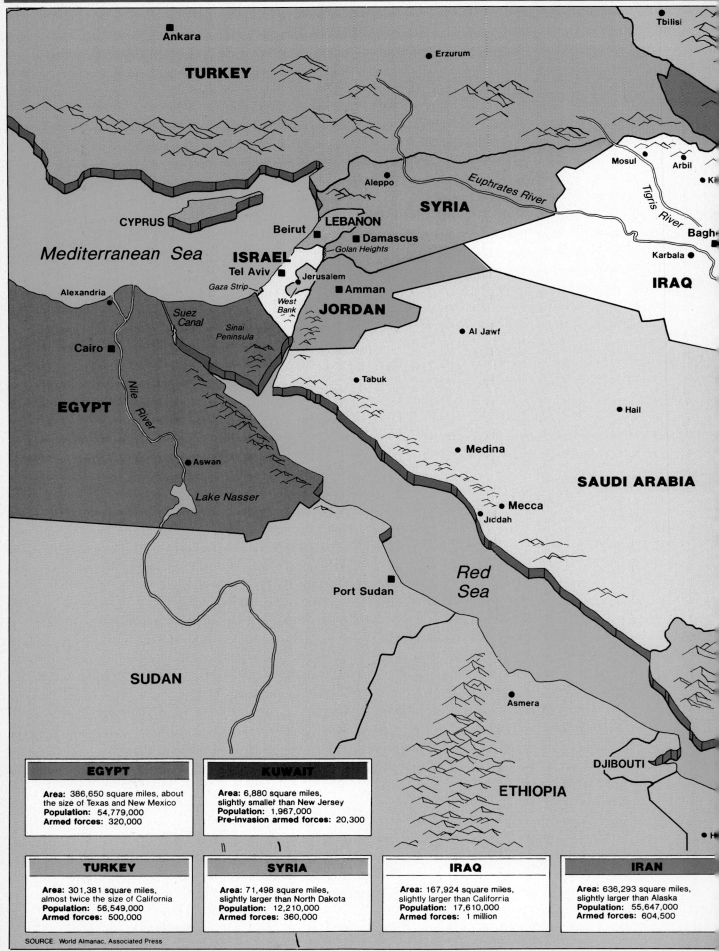

Ankara

TURKEY

Erzurum

Tbilisi

CYPRUS

Mediterranean Sea

Aleppo

Euphrates River

SYRIA

Mosul

Arbil

Ki

Tigris River

Beirut

LEBANON

Damascus

Bagh

ISRAEL

Golan Heights

Tel Aviv

Jerusalem

Karbala

Amman

IRAQ

Gaza Strip

West Bank

JORDAN

Alexandria

Suez Canal

Al Jawf

Sinai Peninsula

Cairo

Tabuk

Hail

EGYPT

Nile River

Medina

SAUDI ARABIA

Aswan

Lake Nasser

Mecca

Jiddah

Red Sea

Port Sudan

SUDAN

Asmera

DJIBOUTI

ETHIOPIA

H

EGYPT

Area: 386,650 square miles, about the size of Texas and New Mexico
Population: 54,779,000
Armed forces: 320,000

KUWAIT

Area: 6,880 square miles, slightly smaller than New Jersey
Population: 1,967,000
Pre-invasion armed forces: 20,300

TURKEY

Area: 301,381 square miles, almost twice the size of California
Population: 56,549,000
Armed forces: 500,000

SYRIA

Area: 71,498 square miles, slightly larger than North Dakota
Population: 12,210,000
Armed forces: 360,000

IRAQ

Area: 167,924 square miles, slightly larger than California
Population: 17,610,000
Armed forces: 1 million

IRAN

Area: 636,293 square miles, slightly larger than Alaska
Population: 55,647,000
Armed forces: 604,500

SOURCE: World Almanac, Associated Press

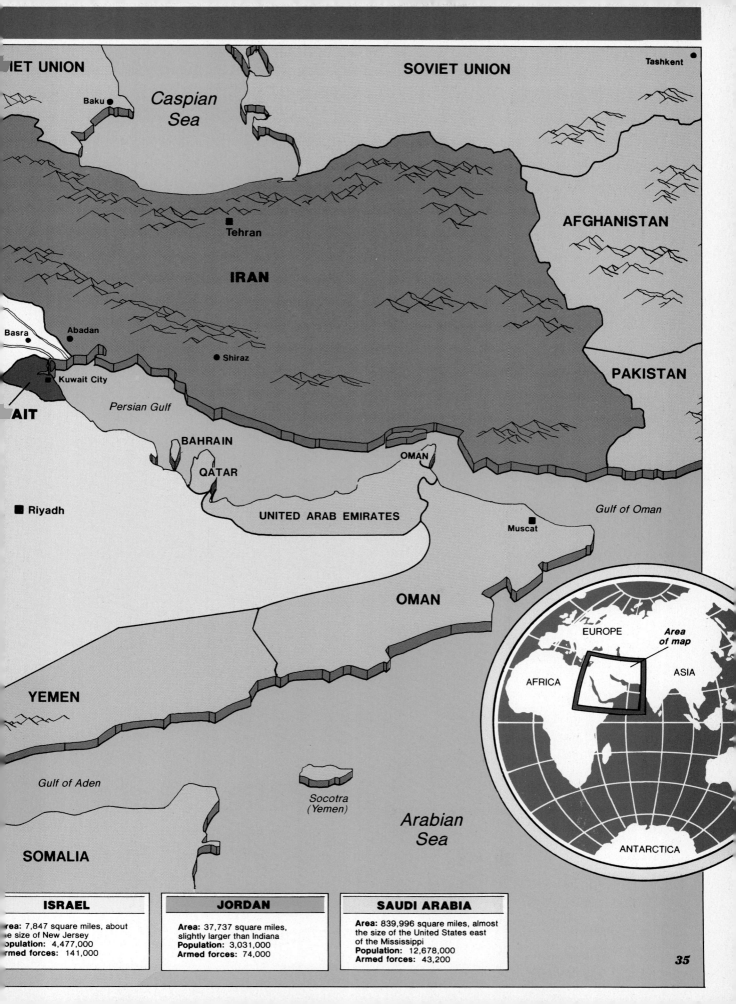

SOVIET UNION

VIET UNION   SOVIET UNION   Tashkent •

Baku •   *Caspian*
            Sea

                                                                              AFGHANISTAN

            ■ Tehran

                    IRAN
                                                                                      PAKISTAN

Basra
        • Abadan
                        • Shiraz

        ■
        Kuwait City
AIT   *Persian Gulf*
                        BAHRAIN

■ Riyadh   QATAR   OMAN

                    UNITED ARAB EMIRATES   *Gulf of Oman*

                                                        ■
                                                        Muscat

                                        OMAN
                                                                EUROPE   *Area
                                                                              of map*

YEMEN   AFRICA   ASIA

Gulf of Aden

                        Socotra
                        (Yemen)   *Arabian
                                        Sea*

SOMALIA
                                                                        ANTARCTICA

ISRAEL	JORDAN	SAUDI ARABIA
rea: 7,847 square miles, about e size of New Jersey **opulation:** 4,477,000 **rmed forces:** 141,000	**Area:** 37,737 square miles, slightly larger than Indiana **Population:** 3,031,000 **Armed forces:** 74,000	**Area:** 839,996 square miles, almost the size of the United States east of the Mississippi **Population:** 12,678,000 **Armed forces:** 43,200

35

F-16 Fighting Falcon ▲

F/A-18 Hornet ▼

Mirage 2000 ▲

◄ *C2/C7 Kfir* ▼

MiG-21 Fishbed ▲

MiG-23 Flogger ▼

MiG-29 Fulcrum

A-6 Intruder ▲

AV-8B Harrier II ▼

A-10 Thunderbolt II ▲ ▼

F-117A Stealth ▲

Jaguar GR.Mk1 ▼

Panavia Tornado ▲

B-52 Stratofortress ▼

F-111 Aardvark ▲

F-4G Wild Weasel ▶

E-3 Sentry (AWACS) ▼

AH-64A Apache

AH-1 HueyCobra ▲

OH-58C Scout ▼

Harpoon missile ▲

◀ *Sidewinder missile* ▼

Sparrow missile ▲

Maverick missile ▶

Phoenix missile ▼

Phoenix
Phoenix Missile System—United States

The six carrier battle groups operating in waters of the Gulf theater of war carry the most sophisticated fighter in history, and one whose longevity may be extended well into the 21st century: the Grumman F-14 Tomcat. Continuously improved since its introduction, the F-14 has assumed a new lease on life as a candidate to replace the canceled A-12 stealth attack plane.

The heart of the Tomcat's unmatched prowess is the combination of its Phoenix missile system and a powerful AWG-9 radar system. A similar combination—of radar and Sidewinder and Sparrow missiles—had proved itself in 1981, and again in 1989, when Libyan planes made the mistake of tangling with American F-14s in the Mediterranean. In the first instance, a pair of Soviet-built Sukhoi 22 attack jets were splashed by Sidewinders; in the second, a pair of more modern, Soviet-built MiG-23 fighters that had been launched at the aircraft carrier USS *John F. Kennedy* were downed by F-14s fielding Sidewinder and Sparrow missiles.

Long-range winner

As impressive as these kills were, the Phoenix missile system possesses capabilities far in excess of that of either Sidewinder or Sparrow. The AWG-9 radar can detect and track up to 24 targets simultaneously, from as low as 50 feet above the surface to above 80,000 feet. The Phoenix's range—better than 120 miles—is unmatched by any other air-launched missile.

The first part of the missile's flight is inertially guided, but

The Phoenix missile is the centerpiece of the F-14's arsenal.

acquires the target on its own homing radar and, from that point, homes in unerringly.

At more than a million dollars apiece, the Phoenix missiles seem extremely expensive, until you realize that the performance they offer is the best protection for a multi-billion-dollar aircraft carrier.

America's aircraft carriers on duty in the Gulf can have no better protection than F-14 Tomcats armed with the unerringly accurate Phoenix missile system.

PHOENIX MISSILE	
Length:	13 ft., 2 in.
Weight:	985 lbs. at launch
Guidance:	Inertial/radar homing
Warhead:	132 lbs.
Range:	120 + miles

Sparrow

Sparrow Missile—United States

America's Desert Storm campaign has been the proving ground for a number of new weapons, notably the Patriot ground-to-air missile. But, as in any armed conflict, much of the burden is assumed by tried-and-true weapons and weapons systems. One of this breed is the AIM-7 Sparrow missile. This venerable air-launched missile has a long development history and a record of constant improvements.

The Sparrow is radar-guided, and the latest versions incorporate a Hercules Mk 58 rocket motor for additional power. The Sparrow can reach a speed of Mach 4, and has a range of more than 60 miles. Highly maneuverable as well as powerful, the Sparrow has been adapted for use as a ship-launched surface-to-air missile.

Smart radar

Continuous-Wave SARH (Semi-Active Radar Homing) guidance allows the Sparrow to distinguish its target from ground clutter. Movable wings allow the missile to adjust its flight by climbing or diving. The AIM-7F improvement has solid-state electronics, which gives added space for the missile's warhead.

The Sparrow is basic air-to-air armament on the F-14 Tomcat and the F-15 Eagle. In service since 1958, the missile is much larger than its contemporary air-to-air missiles, with a length of about 12 feet and a diameter of eight inches.

The Sparrow missile is another old standby that's been showing its stuff in the Desert Storm war. Constantly improved since 1958, it's now carried by American F-14 and F-15 fighters.

Here, the Sparrow missile is mounted further in-wing than the outer Sidewinder.

SPARROW MISSILE

Length:	11 ft., 10 in.
Weight:	504 lbs. at launch
Guidance:	Radar
Warhead:	86 lbs.
Range:	25 miles

Exocet
Exocet Missile—Iraq

The Exocet missile is manufactured by France's SNI Aerospatiale. It is a medium-range air-to-surface or surface-to-surface missile, carrying a 364-pound warhead at near-Mach 1 speed. The Exocet's range is 40 miles.

Bad luck

Although it is a veteran weapon, the sea-skimming Exocet missile has proved itself in two theaters of combat. Argentina used it successfully against the British during the 1981 war in the Falklands, sinking the HMS *Sheffield.* However, in Argentine hands the Exocet was plagued by maintenance failures. Indeed, the *Sheffield* sank not because the Exocet that struck it exploded, but because of a fire that was ignited by the missile's still-burning sustainer rocket. It was reported that other Argentine Exocet hits did not

cause major damage because the missiles had not been properly maintained. At the time of the 1987 Gulf of Hormuz crisis, an Iraqi Exocet severely damaged the USS *Strand.*

Predictably, perhaps, the Iraqis have had little success with the Exocet during the Gulf war, and had much better results with the weapon during the long and costly war with Iran. In that conflict, the large majority of Exocets hit their Iranian targets and detonated successfully.

A French-built Exocet missile is fired from a patrol boat. This extremely effective weapon is the primary antiship missile in Iraq's arsenal.

The French-made Exocet missile was effectively used by Iraq during its war with Iran, but much less successfully in the Gulf war.

EXOCET MISSILE

Length:	15 ft., 4.65 in.
Weight:	1,437 lbs. at launch
Guidance:	Active radar
Warhead:	364 lbs.
Range:	40 + miles

LAND WEAPONRY

With regard to America's involvement in wars past, the advent of hostilities usually found the U.S. Army woefully lacking in manpower, equipment, and training for the task at hand. Operation Desert Storm represents a welcome departure from this tradition of unpreparedness. Indeed, the ground force America deployed for war against Iraq was in many respects the finest army this nation has ever committed to the field of modern-day battle. Although largely untested in actual combat (excepting the veterans of Vietnam and the campaigns in Grenada and Panama), the various elements of this all-volunteer army have been maintained at a peak of readiness, training, and advanced technology.

At the outbreak of Operation Desert Storm, the United States Army had in place in the Saudi Arabian Desert some 245,000 troops, 1,200 main battle tanks, 2,200 armored personnel carriers, and 1,700 helicopters. The Army force was joined by a

Throwing up a plume of sand, an M-60 main battle tank rumbles at speed across desert terrain.

Marine component comprising 75,000 troops and 200 tanks. The combined Army/Marine force was further augmented by 265,000 allied troops, mostly from Britain, France, Saudi Arabia, and Egypt. Arrayed against them were 545,000 Iraqi front-line troops, nearly 500,000 reservists, 4,200 tanks, and 2,800 armored personnel carriers.

M-1 and M-1A1 Abrams
M-1 and M-1A1 Abrams Main Battle Tank—United States

The first M-1 tanks were delivered to the U.S. Army on February 28, 1980. The new tank was named for the late General Creighton W. Abrams, Army Chief of Staff and commander of the 37th Armored Battalion.

Protection against chemical agents

The M-1 mounts a M68E1 105 millimeter main gun. Two 7.62mm NATO M240 machine guns are mounted, one coaxially with the main gun, and one on top of the turret at the loader's satation. A .50 caliber Browning M2 HB machine gun is mounted at the commander's station for antiaircraft defense. The M-1A1, first delivered in August 1985, mounts an M256 120mm smoothbore Rheinmetall main gun developed in West Germany. M-1A1 upgrades also involved more armor protection and a new nuclear-biological-chemical warfare protection system.

The M-1 Abrams hull and turret are built of a material similar to the ceramic and steel plate Chobham armor developed in Britain. The driver is seated in a reclining position in front of the hull; the commander and gunner are in the turret on the right, and the loader is on the left. Armor plate separates the crew compartment from the fuel tanks and ammunition storage.

In March 1988 a program to develop and mount depleted uranium armor plate on the M-1A1 Abrams was instigated; depleted uranium is nonradioactive and is two and a half times as dense as steel. This new armor will raise the total weight of Abrams tanks so equipped to 65 tons.

Immediately following President Bush's decision to commit U.S. forces to Saudi Arabia, American armored units began the difficult process of relocating to the threatened area. The M-1A1's arrival in the theater was accordingly greeted with cries of relief, as it is capable of handling any tank in the Iraqi inventory.

The M-1 Abrams MBT is the U.S. Army's most advanced tank. Tanks provide vital support to ground troops.

There is probably no weapon system whose debut in combat was watched more closely than that of the General Dynamics M-1A1 Abrams tanks.

M-1A1 ABRAMS MAIN BATTLE TANK

Length:	26 ft.
Width:	11 ft., 11 in.
Height:	7 ft., 9.6 in.
Combat weight:	63 tons
Speed:	45 mph
Range:	289 miles
Obstacle/grade performance:	3.5 ft.
Armament:	One 120mm M256 smoothbore main gun Two 7.62mm NATO M240 machine guns One .50 caliber Browning M2 HB machine gun

M-60

M-60 Main Battle Tank—United States

The M-60A3 Main Battle Tank is a vastly improved, more sophisticated fighting vehicle than its predecessors, incorporating the latest laser range-finding equipment and a digital computer.

The M-60 Main Battle Tank carries a variety of ammunition, and its main gun can fire between six and eight rounds per minute.

The M-60 Main Battle Tank (MBT) entered service in 1960 as a replacement for its predecessor, the M-48 Patton Medium Tank. More than 15,000

M-60s of various configurations were built before production ended in August 1987. The latest variant is the M-60A3.

The M-60 hull is built of cast-and-welded sections and divided into three compartments: driving, fighting, and engine/transmission. The turret mounts an L7A1 105 millimeter M68 main gun. Of British design but built in the United States, the main gun is rifled and can fire between six and eight rounds per minute. The tank carries 63 rounds of main gun ammunition. The M-60 also carries two machine guns: a .50 caliber M85 antiaircraft gun in the commander's cupola, and a 7.62mm NATO M73 gun mounted coaxially in the turret.

Laser range finder

A nuclear-biological-chemical warfare protection system was added in the M-60A3 configuration, as well as night vision equipment. It also has an AN/VVG-2 laser range finder connected to an improved fire control system that uses an M21 solid state computer. The new system allows either the gunner or the tank commander to fire the main gun.

The M-60A3 has a track system with replaceable pads. An automatic Halon fire extinguisher system, a smoke-screen system, and the M219 smoke grenade launcher have also been installed. A deep-water fording kit allows an M-60A3 fitted with a snorkel to traverse water up to 13 feet deep. Most of the General Dynamics-built M-60A3s have been updated with reactive armor, essential against Saddam Hussein's forces.

M-60A3 MAIN BATTLE TANK

Length:	22 ft., 7 in.
Width:	11 ft., 9.6 in.
Height:	10 ft., 8 in.
Combat weight:	58 tons
Speed:	30 mph
Range:	298 miles
Obstacle/grade performance:	2.9 ft.
Armament:	One 105mm L7A1 main gun
	One 7.62mm NATO M73 machine gun
	One .50 caliber M85 machine gun

Challenger
Challenger Main Battle Tank—Britain

The Challenger Main Battle Tank (MBT) became operational in 1983. Like its predecessor, the Chieftain, the Challenger is an accommodation of firepower, armor protection, and speed and agility. The turret and hull are protected by Chobham armor and steel plate armor. Chobham armor is a compound of plastic, ceramic, and steel plates designed to absorb and deflect kinetic rounds and protect against shaped-charge gas plasma jets.

The Challenger's main armament is the 120 millimeter L11A5 rifled gun. It is also armed with two 7.62mm NATO machine guns, one mounted coaxially with the main gun, the other near the commander's cupola for antiaircraft defense.

The Challenger has a gunnery and sighting system that incorporates a laser range finder and a thermal imaging system for use at night, in smoke, or in fog. A new gun sighting system known as TOGS—Thermal Observation and Gunnery System—is now being installed in all Challenger tanks.

Slow but formidable
The Challenger's fire control system does not seem to be as accurate or as fast as that of the M-1 Abrams. Evidently, the TOGS sight cannot scan independently of the turret's own movement. This reduces the commander's ability to search for new targets while the gunner fires on the current target. The Challenger is also fairly slow in comparison to American and Soviet MBTs. Nevertheless, the Challenger is in most respects a formidable tank, inasmuch as it is far more heavily armed and armored

Thick armor and a hard-hitting 120mm gun are the hallmarks of Britain's superb Challenger Main Battle Tank.

than its counterparts. And it is certain that British soldiers, in writing yet another chapter in their long history of desert warfare, are justly proud of their main battle tank's capabilities.

It is fascinating to think what Monty's World War II "Desert Rats" would have done against Rommel with a few divisions of tanks like the Vickers Defense Systems Challenger.

CHALLENGER MAIN BATTLE TANK

Length:	27 ft., 5 in.
Width:	11 ft., 3 in.
Height:	8 ft., 2 in.
Combat weight:	68.3 tons
Speed:	35 mph
Range:	250 miles
Obstacle/grade performance:	3.0 ft.
Armament:	One 120mm 55 caliber L115A rifled gun
	Two 7.62mm NATO machine guns

T-72

T-72 Main Battle Tank—Iraq

The 90,000-pound T-72, with its enormous 125mm smoothbore gun, is in keeping with a Soviet tradition, begun in World War II against the Germans, of fielding heavily armed and armored main battle tanks.

In Iraqi hands, the superb capabilities of the Soviet-built T-72 Main Battle Tank were compromised by the decision to use them in a fixed "fortress" role.

Production of the T-72 Main Battle Tank (MBT) is thought to have started in 1972. The T-72 is well protected by 11-inch armor on the turret face and 8.8 inches of spaced, laminate armor on the hull nose, which is angled to provide the equivalent of 21.5 inches of armor.

The tank mounts a 125 millimeter smoothbore Model 2A465 main gun, which is fed from an automatic carousel loader mounted on the hull floor. The main gun is stabilized, allowing the T-72 to shoot on the move. A 7.62mm machine gun is mounted in the turret coaxially with the main gun and can be fired automatically. A 12.7mm DShKM machine gun is mounted ahead of the hatch on the commander's cupola.

Radiation protection

The T-72 mounts an infrared searchlight on the right side of the main gun. It also carries a snorkel clipped to the left side of the turret, and has full nuclear-biological-chemical protection. The interior of the tank is also lined with a lead-impregnated material for protection against radiation and neutron pulses.

Israeli tanks operating in Lebanon in 1982 destroyed a large number of Syrian-manned T-72s. Since then, the Soviets have enhanced the tank's survivability with the installation of applique armor, fender skirts, and reaction armor boxes.

To date, an estimated 17,000 T-72 tanks have been built. In addition to Iraq, the T-72 has been distributed to 14 nations in Eastern Europe, the Middle East, and Africa. Iraq's initial deployment of its 500-odd T-72 tanks was highly conservative, digging them in the familiar triangular "forts" that were developed in the war with Iran.

T-72 MAIN BATTLE TANK

Length:	22 ft., 7 in.
Width:	11 ft., 9.5 in.
Height:	7 ft., 8.5 in.
Combat weight:	45.2 tons
Speed:	37 mph
Range:	298 miles
Obstacle/grade performance:	3.0 ft.
Armament:	One 125mm 2A465 smoothbore main gun
	One 7.62mm PKT machine gun
	One 12.7mm DShKM machine gun

T-62

T-62 Main Battle Tank—Iraq

Production on the T-62 Main Battle Tank (MBT) began in 1962, and an estimated 20,000 were built during the next eight years. The T-62's main gun is the 115 millimeter U-5TS smoothbore. One 7.62mm PKT machine gun is mounted coaxially, and a 12.7mm DShKM machine gun is mounted on the turret for antiaircraft defense.

The T-62's turret is cast in one piece and is 9.5 inches thick on its forward face. The T-62 and T-62A have been updated with a laser range finder, a solid-state ballistic computer, new infrared driving and searchlights, and an image intensifier for night work. Appliqué and reaction armor have also been installed on some T-62s.

The T-62 has a nuclear radiation protection system that automatically seals the tank when a preset level of radiation is encountered. A blower and filtration system removes radiation-contaminated dust and other particles. There is no biological or chemical protection system, and the crew must wear contamination suits.

More tanks than Hitler

The T-62 has several flaws. Its main gun cannot be aimed low enough to deal with attacking infantry, and its rate of fire is slowed by a complicated fire control system. Moreover, the main gun elevates after recoil, and the turret cannot be traversed during the loading sequence. Consequently, the T-62 was consistently defeated by Israeli tanks during the 1973 Yom Kippur War and the 1982 invasion of Lebanon. Despite its drawbacks, however, it is used by some 23 countries. Prior to the Desert Storm operations,

A T-62 displays the low profile and rounded turret so typical of Soviet Main Battle Tanks. The exposed fuel tanks on the rear could prove a hazardous liability in combat.

Iraq had more than 1,000 T-62As in its inventory—far more than the number of heavy tanks that Hitler's armies used in their 1940 blitzkrieg against Western Europe.

The T-62A has a very low silhouette, which makes tracking it difficult. But it lacks adequate armor protection, as Soviet crews in Afghanistan discovered to their dismay.

T-62 MAIN BATTLE TANK

Length:	21 ft., 8.5 in.
Width:	10 ft., 9.5 in.
Height:	7 ft., 9.5 in.
Combat weight:	44 tons
Speed:	31 mph
Range:	279 miles
Obstacle/grade performance:	2.6 ft.
Armament:	One 115mm U-5TS smoothbore main gun
	One 7.62mm PKT machine gun
	One 12.7mm DShKM machine gun

M2/M3 Bradley

M2/M3 Bradley Infantry and Cavalry Fighting Vehicles —United States

The M2 Bradley Fighting Vehicle can keep pace with main battle tanks, carrying the infantry troops needed to support tank operations.

Selected for use in 1976, the M2/M3 Bradley fighting vehicle was designed specifically to carry troops, protect tanks, conduct mounted warfare, and consolidate gains made by armor.

The Bradley weighs 25 tons and is capable of traveling 41 miles per hour on a hard surface. With its tracks providing propulsion in the water, the Bradley can swim at a speed of 4.2 miles per hour. The vehicle's cruising range is 300 miles. It can pivot on its own axis, climb 60-degree slopes, cross 40-degree slopes, climb 36-inch walls, and cross trenches 100 inches wide.

Accuracy on rough terrain

The M2 Infantry Fighting Vehicle (IFV) and the M3 Cavalry Fighting Vehicle (CFV) are both armed with a turret-mounted M242 25 millimeter chain gun. The M242 can be fired accurately while the vehicle is moving at speed over rough terrain. An M240C coaxial machine gun is mounted to the right of the main gun. Additional armament includes seven TOW missiles fired from a launcher mounted on the left side of the turret. The TOWs are capable of defeating Soviet main battle tanks at an extreme range of 3,000 yards.

The M2 IFV carries a nine-man infantry squad, as well as six ball-mounted M231 Colt 5.56mm, port-firing automatic weapons. The infantry troops can fight from inside the Bradley, then quickly exit to fight outside the vehicle. The M3 CFV has a crew of five, carries more 25mm ammunition than the IFV, and has 10 additional TOWs. In open terrain such as that encountered in the Desert Storm operations, the Bradley can significantly reduce casualties even as it helps to further offensive capability.

M2/M3 BRADLEY INFANTRY AND CAVALRY FIGHTING VEHICLES

Length:	21 ft., 2 in.
Width:	10 ft., 6 in.
Height:	9 ft., 9 in.
Weight:	49,802 lbs.
Speed:	41 mph
Range:	300 miles
Obstacle/grade performance:	3.0 ft.
Armament:	One 25mm chain gun
	One 7.62mm machine gun
	One twin launcher for TOW missiles

M998 (HMMWV)

M998 High Mobility, Multi-purpose Wheeled Vehicle (HMMWV) —United States

The HMMWV is a 1¼-ton, four-wheel drive, multi-faceted utility vehicle designed to fill a variety of military roles for modern ground forces. Popularly known as the HummVee, or Hummer, it was adopted by the U.S. armed forces in 1982 to replace the aging series of Jeep vehicles. It can also supplant the M274 half-ton MULE, the 1¼-ton M880 pickup truck, and the M792 1¼-ton ambulance in their respective roles. A low silhouette profile and high maneuvering rate allow the Hummer to offer much greater flexibility in terms of battlefield movement than the vehicles it replaces.

A multifunctional vehicle

At least 60,000 Hummers have been delivered to the U.S. Army, Air Force, and Marines. The Hummer family of vehicles consists of up to 18 different variations. Mounting TOW missile systems, the Hummer can function in a tank-busting "shoot and scoot" role. It can also be armed with 7.62 millimeter and .50 caliber machine guns, and the MK 19 grenade launcher system. Additionally, the Hummer can provide battlefield assistance as a staff car, supply wagon, troop carrier, communications center, command post, medical evacuation vehicle, and weapons carrier.

All Hummers have the same chassis, engine, and transmission for ease of repair and maintenance. Although still in the early stages of its service career, in the trackless wastes so typical of Operation Desert Storm the Hummer has already proved itself a tough combat

The Hummer (HMMWV) has replaced the Jeep as the Army's everyday utility vehicle. A range of weaponry, including a variety of rockets, can be attached to the Hummer.

vehicle that gets troops in and out of harm's way quickly, and with a high degree of survivability.

The M998 "Hummer" is to the Jeep what the F-15 is to the Mustang: faster, more powerful, and infinitely more capable.

M998 HIGH MOBILITY, MULTIPURPOSE WHEELED VEHICLE (HMMWV)

Length:	15 ft.
Width:	7 ft., 1 in.
Height:	5 ft., 7.5 in.
Weight:	4,969 lbs.
Wheelbase:	10 ft., 8 in.
Speed:	65 mph
Range:	351 miles

M198 Howitzer

M198 155mm Towed Howitzer—United States

In countering the Soviet (hence, Iraqi) philosophy of big guns, and lots of them, the U.S. brought to bear the M198 155mm howitzer, a towed gun of tremendous range and versatility.

Allied forces counter Iraq's superiority in artillery with the M198 Howitzer.

First production models of the M198 Howitzer were delivered to the U.S. Army and Marine Corps in 1978. It is expected that the M198 will be America's

towed field artillery piece for many years to come.

The M198 can be lifted by the CH-47 and CH-53E helicopters, prime movers respectively of the Army and Marine Corps. The M939 five-ton truck is the weapon's other prime mover. The M198 and its recoil mechanism are mounted on a split-trail carriage. The carriage wheels are mounted on a two-position suspension system so that the wheels can be lifted up and out of contact with the ground by a hand-operated hydraulic pump. In the firing position, the M198 sits solidly on its firing platform without having to be anchored, and its long trails are opened into a wide "V". The cannon itself is transported either with the barrel forward or rotated to rest aft along the trails.

Less than five minutes to fire

The M198's gun tube is fitted with a screw-on, double-baffle muzzle brake. The barrel can be elevated by hand to an angle of 71 degrees for firing at close range, and it can be depressed to five degrees below centerline for transporting or for point-blank firing. The gun fires a full range of U.S. separate-loading 155 millimeter ammunition, and a trained crew of 11 needs less than five minutes to tow the M198 into position and ready it for firing.

If there was one area where the Iraqi army possessed clear superiority at the outbreak of the conflict, it was in artillery. Yet U.S. artillery batteries, while not nearly so numerous, could nevertheless consider themselves well-armed with the excellent M198.

M198 155mm TOWED HOWITZER

Length:	
Barrel:	20 ft.
Overall:	40 ft., 5.8 in. (traveling)
Width:	
Traveling:	9.16 ft.
Firing:	28 ft.
Weight:	15,791.4 lbs.
Recoil system:	Hydropneumatic
Carriage:	Split-trail
Rate of fire:	
Maximum:	Four rounds per minute for 3 minutes
Sustained:	Two rounds per minute
Range (conventional ammunition):	24,059 yds.

M109 Howitzer

M109 155mm Self-propelled Howitzer—United States

The M109 self-propelled 155 millimeter howitzer is the standard direct support artillery weapon in U.S. armored and mechanized infantry units. It carries a crew of six: commander, gunner, driver, and three ammunition handlers. The driver sits in the left front portion of the hull, with the engine to his right. Command and gunnery stations are in the turret. The hull and turret are built of welded aluminum. The armor, also aluminum, is reinforced with Kevlar anti-spalling liners. The M109A2/3 turret has a full-width bustle that carries 22 rounds of 155mm ammunition.

A 155mm main gun

The M109A2/3 can maintain a road speed of 33 miles per hour, and ford streams as deep as six feet at four miles per hour. The main armament is the 16.66-foot M185 155 millimeter cannon, which fires a conventional high-explosive round to a range of 19,794 yards. When firing a rocket-assisted projectile, the M109A2/3 can achieve ranges up to 26,246 yards. The gun can fire one round per minute or, for short periods, three rounds per minute. The gun tube can be elevated to 75 degrees, depressed five degrees below centerline, and traversed 360 degrees. All gun controls are hydraulic and have manual backup. The M109A2/3 can fire a complete range of U.S. 155mm ammunition, including high-explosive, smoke, illumination, tactical nuclear, chemical, and rocket-assisted high-explosive rounds. Secondary armament is a .50 caliber M2 heavy-barrel machine gun

M109 Self-propelled Howitzers saw plenty of training for desert warfare during Operation Bright Star exercises in Egypt.

mounted on the turret near the commander's station.

All told, the M109 is a highly mobile weapon perfectly suited to providing artillery support in the fast-changing conditions of armored warfare in the desert.

Operation Desert Storm was not the first time the M109 has seen combat. As a vital component of the Israeli armed forces, this self-propelled howitzer has more than demonstrated its worth in a shooting war in the Middle East.

M109 155mm SELF-PROPELLED HOWITZER

Length:	
Barrel:	16 ft., 8 in.
Overall:	29 ft., 11 in.
Width:	10 ft., 4 in.
Weight:	55,000 lbs.
Speed:	33 mph
Recoil system:	Hydropneumatic
Rate of fire:	
Maximum:	Three rounds per minute
Sustained:	One round per minute
Range (conventional ammunition):	19,794 yds.

M163 Vulcan

M163 Vulcan Self-propelled Air-Defense System—United States

The Vulcan six-barrel gun has a terrifying rate of fire that can result in the utter annihilation of any infantry force it might catch in an exposed position. As an anti-aircraft weapon, how-ever, the Vulcan leaves much to be desired.

The Vulcan Air-Defense System entered service in 1968.

In the past, infantry soldiers were often drilled not to leave the road and hide when attacked by strafing aircraft, but instead to stand and fire as rapidly as possible so as to throw a curtain of bullets in front of the diving planes. The M163 recalls that most basic method of antiaircraft work—although by several orders of magnitude.

Using the versatile M113A1 Armored Personnel Carrier as the vehicle, the Vulcan consists of a one-man power-operated turret with a range-only VPS-2 radar, an M-52 gyro lead computing sight developed by Lockheed, and the M61A1 Vulcan 20 millimeter six-barrel cannon. Somewhat in reverse of the usual procedure, the operator first acquires the target visually, and then the radar unit calculates the range to the target.

Two rates of fire

The Vulcan gun was originally developed by General Electric as an aircraft cannon, and saw service initially on the Lockheed F-104 Starfighter. The six-barrel 20mm cannon has two rates of fire—1,000 rounds per minute for use against ground forces, and 3,000 rounds per minute for use against aircraft.

The Vulcan earned its stripes in Vietnam, where it was used for protecting vehicle convoys. When the Viet Cong ambushed a column, American soldiers were comforted to have the Vulcan provide suppressing fire.

Unfortunately, the Vulcan does not have an all-weather capability, severely limiting its utility in most areas of the world. This was not so much a problem in the Persian Gulf war as it might have been in the not infrequently troublesome weather conditions that prevail in more northerly climes. Economy moves have elimi-nated proposed successors, so the Vulcan will likely be a mainstay of U.S. Army forces for many more years.

M163 VULCAN SELF-PROPELLED AIR-DEFENSE SYSTEM

Length:	16 ft.
Width:	9 ft., 4 in.
Height:	9 ft.
Weight:	27,000 lbs.
Speed:	43 mph

Lance

Lance Battlefield Support Missile (MGM-52C)—United States

The Lance Battlefield Support Missile, which is issued at corps level, is a general support weapon for use against rear enemy positions. Like most U.S. weapons in the Gulf war, it was the product of a fruitful cooperation between several contractors, with LTV being prime. Mobile and easily moved, the missile and launcher can be quickly moved to a new position to avoid counterbattery fire.

Immune to countermeasures

The Lance guidance system is self-contained; before launching, the location of the missile is entered into the guidance system, along with meteorological data at the launch and impact points. The missile is then guided in-flight by a directional-control and automatic meteorological compensation system known as DC-AUTOMET. The guidance system is virtually immune to electronic countermeasures.

The Lance uses a hypergolic fuel that ignites spontaneously in the presence of an oxidizer. While in flight, the Lance is stabilized via spinning, which is accomplished by venting propulsion gases through control vents just forward of the missile's midline.

The Lance is transported on the M752 vehicle, a specially adapted version of the M113 Armored Personnel Carrier that has been fitted as a launching vehicle. Another vehicle, the M688, carries two complete Lance missiles for reloading.

With a 1,000-pound conventional high-explosive submunition warhead (M251), Lance has a range of up to 43 miles. The M251 warhead is filled with 836 BLU-63 anti-personnel/

The Lance missile supports ground troops by attacking enemy rear positions such as airfields and second-echelon enemy troop concentrations.

anti-materiel bomblets. When equipped with the W70 Mod 1 or Mod 2 nuclear warhead weighing 465 pounds and yielding ten kilotons, or the W70 Mod 4 neutron warhead, the Lance's range is 75 miles.

One of the most important of the NATO battlefield support systems, the Lance liquid-fuel rocket with a conventional warhead weighs almost 4,000 pounds and has a range of 43 miles.

LANCE BATTLEFIELD SUPPORT MISSILE (MGM-52C)

Length:	20 ft., 3 in.
Diameter:	1 ft., 10 in.
Weight:	3,920 lbs. at launch
Speed:	Supersonic
Range with warhead:	
Conventional:	43 miles
Nuclear:	75 miles

Multiple Launch Rocket System

Multiple Launch Rocket System (MLRS)—United States

Designed to replace conventional tube artillery, the MLRS can lay down a devastating blanket of fire against a designated target area.

The Multiple Launch Rocket System, like the Lance, is designed to strike far in enemy rear areas.

The Multiple Launch Rocket System (MLRS), developed by LTV for the U.S. Army and Marine Corps, is intended to strike far into the rear of armored forces. It had a perfect target in the entrenched, triangular fortresses the Iraqis created to withstand Operation Desert Storm. The MLRS consists of a launcher, free rockets, a computerized aim and control complex, and a tracked vehicle. The system is capable of launching within one minute from one to 12 rockets to a range of 18 miles.

Bradley provides transport

The system's tracked Armored Vehicle Mounted Rocket Launcher (AVMRL) is built on the same chassis as the M2 Bradley Infantry Fighting Vehicle. The AVMRL has a range of 300 miles, a top speed of 40 miles per hour, and considerable off-road capability. The Launcher Loader Module is bolted to the vehicle bed and can be raised to 60 degrees and traversed in a complete circle. Two boom-mounted electrical cable hoists can be used by crew members to reload the two rocket pod/containers.

The MLRS rocket is a tube-launched, free-flight vehicle weighing approximately 667 pounds. It is 12.9 feet long and 8.9 inches in diameter. Inside the warhead are polyurethane foam containers holding 644 individual M77 anti-personnel/anti-materiel submunitions effective against personnel and light armor. When the MLRS rocket reaches the target area, a black-powder charge in the center of the warhead is detonated by a timer and the submunitions are expelled in a circular or oval pattern, depending on the range. Each submunition is stabilized by a ribbon parachute as it falls, and explodes on contact.

MULTIPLE LAUNCH ROCKET SYSTEM (MLRS)

Length:	12 ft., 11 in. per rocket
Diameter:	8.9 in. per rocket
Weight:	667 lbs. per rocket
Vehicle speed:	40 mph
Rate of fire:	12 rockets in 1 minute
Range:	
Rocket:	18 miles
Vehicle:	300 miles

M-1A1 Abrams ▲

M-60 A3 ▼

Challenger ▲

T-72 ▼

T-62 ▲

Bradley Fighting Vehicle ▼

M998 HMMWV

M198 Towed Howitzer

M109 Self-propelled Howitzer ▲ | M163 Vulcan ▼ | Lance missile ▶

Multiple Launch Rocket ▲▼
System (MLRS)

Chaparral missile ▲

Hawk missile ▼

Patriot missile ▲ ▼

FIM-92A Stinger ▲

◀ *Scud missile*

Chemical/Biological Weapons ▲

◀ Nimitz-*class aircraft carrier* Iowa-*class battleship* ▲ Virginia-*class cruiser* ▼

Spruance-*class destroyer* ▲

Oliver Hazard Perry-*class frigate* ▼

Tactical Missile System

Tactical Missile System (TACMS)—United States

The Tactical Missile System (TACMS) uses the same launch and guidance support equipment as the MLRS. The TACMS missile is also the same length as the MLRS missile. However, the TACMS missile has a longer range and a wider diameter; and, unlike the ballistic-trajectory, free-flight MLRS rocket, the TACMS missile is guided to its target by a unit employing a ring-laser gyro guidance system.

The TACMS launcher carries one missile per pod. The TACMS missile uses an Arcadene 360 solid rocket motor; four movable tail fins provide maneuvering ability and stabilization in flight. The warhead carries a classified number of M74 anti-personnel/anti-materiel grenades.

TACMS uses the M270 tracked launcher, which is built on the M2 Bradley Infantry Fighting Vehicle chassis. TACMS carries a crew of three: driver, gunner, and section chief. The launcher weighs 25 tons, is 23 feet long, 8.2 feet high, and 9.5 feet wide. TACMS can reach a maximum speed of 40 miles per hour and has excellent cross-country ability.

Fire control by computer

The guidance system, carried on the M270, consists of a computerized fire control system, on board stabilization reference package, a position-determining system, and a built-in reloading system. The position-determining system receives signals from the Department of Defense's navigation satellites to pinpoint its location anywhere in the world. The reloading mechanism enables the crew to draw

Artist's rendering of a TACMS in operation. The missile system is depicted in the concealment of a tree grove, a luxury not available to the troops of Operation Desert Storm.

reloads from a supply vehicle without leaving the armored launcher.

In conditions like those encountered in Kuwait, the non-nuclear TACMS gains lethality by dispensing terminally guided submunitions over a wide battlefield area.

The success of the MLRS positioned Vought to secure the contract for the follow-on Army Tactical Missile System (TACMS), a non-nuclear replacement for its own Lance missile.

TACTICAL MISSILE SYSTEM (TACMS)

Length:	12 ft., 11 in. per rocket
Diameter:	2 ft. per rocket
Weight:	Classified
Vehicle speed:	40 mph
Rate of fire:	Classified
Range:	
Rocket:	60 miles
Vehicle:	300 miles

M-109 (TOW)

M-109 Improved Tube-launched, Optically Tracked, Wire-guided (TOW) Missile—United States

An American soldier trains with an original TOW. The M-109 Improved TOW carries a more powerful explosive.

The TOW operator watches as a 60-ton tank grinds toward him, confident that he can destroy the attacking steel behemoth with one press of a button.

The M-109 Improved TOW is a direct descendant of the World War II-era bazooka. Manufactured by Hughes under the designation BGM-71C, the Improved TOW represents significant enhancement of the TOW weapons that were first introduced in 1970. In Operation Desert Storm it was used as a hand-held weapon, on armored vehicles, and on helicopters.

To use, the operator centers the target in the cross hairs of the 13x optical sight. The operator presses the firing button to ignite a rocket, which pops the missile from its launch container. To protect the TOW crew from injury, all fuel is consumed before the missile leaves the tube. At a distance of 120 feet, the smokeless sustainer motor ignites and the warhead arms. Before the sustainer motor accelerates the missile to 900 feet per second, four large wings unfold to provide lift. Combustion then stops and the missile glides to its target, two thin wires trailing behind.

Sending commands by joystick

The missile is steered by the operator, who watches through the launcher sight and uses a joystick to correct the missile's flight path. A sensor on the launcher watches the flare at the missile's base, computes the angular distance between the flare in the sight and the sight center, and automatically transmits correction signals along the trailing wires. Impact speed at the maximum range of 4,000 yards is greater than 225 miles per hour. The Improved TOW's warhead is fitted with a standoff probe that causes an explosion some 15 inches from the armor plate to enhance penetration.

TOW became operational in 1970 with the United States and West German armies. Well over 600,000 TOWs have been manufactured. In Operation Desert Storm it was used as a hand-held weapon, on armored vehicles, and on helicopters.

M-109 IMPROVED TUBE-LAUNCHED, OPTICALLY TRACKED, WIRE-GUIDED (TOW) MISSILE (BGM-71C)

Length:	5 ft., 1 in.
Diameter:	6 in.
Weight:	57 lbs.
Speed:	625 mph
Range:	4,000 yds.

Chaparral

M48A1 Chaparral Low-Altitude Self-propelled Surface-to-Air Missile System—United States

The Chaparral is a low-altitude air-defense system developed to protect troops in the Forward Edge of the Battle Area (FEBA) from enemy aircraft. The missile itself is a refinement of the Sidewinder air-to-air missile. In trained hands, it is more than a match for the Soviet-designed and built aircraft employed by Saddam Hussein's air force.

Development of the Chaparral system began in 1964, with the first production versions delivered to the U.S. Army in 1969. The system employs a heat-seeking missile designed for use against high-performance aircraft flying at low altitudes to attack troops. The missile itself is five inches in diameter and 9.5 inches long, and has four fixed wings and movable control surfaces aft.

Fired and forgotten

The missile is equipped with smokeless rocket motors to reduce infrared signature, and it has fire-and-forget capability. This means that, once launched, the missile is on its own, continuing to track and guide itself toward the enemy aircraft, using its onboard infrared heat-seeking sensors. The missile's M250 warhead contains a proximity fuse. At a specified (and classified) distance, the warhead explodes. A high explosive turns the missile warhead and the explosive case into shrapnel.

The system is normally mounted on the M730A2 tracked carrier, with four missiles carried on a railed launcher. Eight more missiles are contained in special storage compartments in the vehicle.

The launch control station is comprised of a collapsible crew cab and missile-launching turret. The unarmored M730 provides power to run all electrical systems; it does not provide nuclear-biological-chemical (NBC) protection for its crew.

The Chaparral Surface-to-Air Missile System—which entered service in 1969—is usually deployed in company with the Vulcan.

M48A1 CHAPARRAL LOW-ALTITUDE SELF-PROPELLED SURFACE-TO-AIR MISSILE SYSTEM

Vehicle:	M730A2
Length:	19 ft., 11 in.
Width:	8 ft., 9.5 in.
Weight:	28,712.5 lbs.
Speed:	38 mph
Range:	313 miles
Armament:	Twelve Chaparral AA missiles
Length:	9 ft., 6 in.
Diameter:	5 in.
Weight:	185 lbs.
Altitude:	19,685 ft.
Speed:	Mach 2.5
Range:	3.78 miles

Hawk

MIM-23B Hawk Air-Defense Missile System —United States

against attacking aircraft flying at altitudes between 15,000 and 60,000 feet. Hawk is powered by a solid-fuel rocket motor, and carries a warhead with a proximity fuse and a 120-pound high-explosive charge. Upon detonation, the explosion fragments the surrounding casing and destroys the target with shrapnel.

A noisy weapon

The Hawk missile launcher is mounted on the self-propelled M727 launcher unit. The entire system, though heavy, is air-transportable. A typical Hawk battery consists of six three-round launchers; a tracked loading vehicle carrying three rounds; a pulse-acquisition radar unit to acquire medium-altitude enemy aircraft; continuous wave acquisition radar (which searches for low-altitude enemy intruders); two target-illuminating radars; a range-only radar that measures the distance to the target on a real-time basis and then supplies that distance to the continuous wave radars; and the battery control center. By modern standards, the Hawk battery is "noisy" in the electronic sense, making it a target for enemy aircraft equipped to detect and destroy radar installations.

The Hawk has undergone numerous upgrades and improvements throughout its service career. Despite its bulk and complexity, the Mach 2.5 Hawk missile remains one of the best air-defense systems in the world for medium-altitude interdiction. Unfortunately, the Hawk was furnished to Kuwait, where many were captured by Iraqi forces—thus posing a threat to United Nations aircraft.

Although the Hawk is somewhat large, heavy, and cumbersome by 1990s standards, the U.S. Department of Defense decided in 1982 to keep the system in service until after the turn of the century.

The Hawk is one of the oldest antiaircraft missile systems still in active service with U.S. forces.

Hawk (Homing-All-the-Way-Killer) was developed by the Raytheon Company in the mid-1950s, and first deployed by the U.S. Army in 1960. It is a surface-to-air guided missile designed to provide protection

MIM-23B HAWK AIR-DEFENSE MISSILE SYSTEM

Length:	16 ft., 6 in.
Diameter:	1 ft., 2 in.
Weight:	1,382 lbs.
Speed:	Mach 2.5
Range:	25 miles
Altitude:	15,000 to 60,000 ft.

MIM-104 Patriot

MIM-104 Patriot Tactical Air-Defense Missile System —United States

The MIM-104 Patriot air-defense system, while pushing the limits of state-of-the-art, experienced several setbacks and cost overruns during development. But all the problems were solved, and the Patriot now works exactly as designed and provides excellent value.

Shrapnel destroys the target

The Patriot is designed to defend against medium- to high-altitude high-performance aircraft and ballistic missiles. The system employs a 17.4-foot-long missile powered by a solid-propellant rocket motor at Mach 3 speeds. Armed with a high-explosive warhead that is detonated by a proximity fuse, the Patriot destroys its target with shrapnel.

The missile is carried in a storage/transportation container that serves as the launcher. Four Patriot missiles in containers are mounted on the M-901 launch station, which is attached to the M-860 trailer. The engagement control station (MSQ-104) is mounted on an M-818 tractor and contains all the necessary command and control equipment. Another trailer, parked a short distance from the M-860 trailer and M-818 tractor, houses subsidiary ground control radar.

The Track Via Missile (TVM) guidance system is the heart of the system, and accounts for its great accuracy. The Patriot missile system is so versatile that it can track and steer eight missiles to different targets at the same time, with any three in the TVM stage of flight.

In Operation Desert Storm, Patriot missiles racked up a near-miraculous kill ratio against Iraqi Scud missiles. The first of

The redoubtable Patriot missile system may not look like much, but there can no doubt as to its effectiveness against Iraq's Scud missiles.

many such kills occurred on Friday, January 18, 1991, at 4:28 a.m., when a Patriot missile destroyed an attacking Scud over eastern Saudi Arabia. This incident marked the first time an anti-missile missile had been used successfully in combat.

In the past, the Patriot missile system was often maligned as a costly boondoggle. Yet its stunning successes in intercepting incoming Iraqi Scud missiles during Operation Desert Storm has earned it the respect of military analysts, as well as the soldiers and civilians it was charged with defending.

MIM-104 PATRIOT TACTICAL AIR-DEFENSE MISSILE SYSTEM

Length:	17 ft., 5 in.
Diameter:	1 ft., 4 in.
Weight:	2,200 lbs.
Range:	42.5 miles
Altitude:	79,000 ft.
Speed:	Mach 3

FIM-92A Stinger

FIM-92A Stinger—United States

An American soldier prepares to launch a Stinger. This hand-held antiaircraft system was largely responsible for the Soviet withdrawal from Afghanistan.

The FIM-92A Stinger provides infantry soldiers with a weapon to protect vital installations as well as their own formations. It can also be adapted for use on helicopters and fixed wing aircraft.

Few hand-held weapons are ever considered to have a war-winning capability, but the success of the General Dynamics FIM-92A Stinger in Afghanistan is widely regarded as a primary reason for the Soviet withdrawal from that country.

A lightweight system

The Stinger is a one-man, portable, shoulder-launched, antiaircraft rocket. The Stinger missile is five and a half feet long, and is launched from a reusable, hand-gripped launcher that contains the Identification Friend or Foe (IFF) system antenna. The entire system weighs less than 35 pounds.

To fire the Stinger, the operator arms the weapon and clips the IFF unit to his belt; the IFF's electrical cord is attached to the launcher unit. When an enemy aircraft appears, the operator lifts the launcher unit to his shoulder and sights the target through an open, or iron sight, system which resembles a three-sided box. The soldier activates the missile's infrared sensor while pointing the launcher at the target. When the sensor has detected and locked onto the enemy aircraft's engine exhaust, the soldier hears a high-pitched, steady tone. The IFF system is used to interrogate the enemy aircraft. If the response is not positive, the soldier pulls the trigger.

The missile is powered by a dual-thrust, solid-fuel rocket motor at Mach 2 speed. Eight control surfaces, four at the nose and four at the tail, "pop up" from the missile's fuselage. The infrared seeker in the missile's nose continues to home in on the target's exhaust plume, providing flight path steering corrections to the missile's guidance command system. The Stinger missile is fitted with a hit-to-kill warhead that detonates 6.6 pounds of high explosive to destroy the enemy aircraft.

FIM-92A STINGER	
Length:	5 ft., 6 in.
Diameter:	2.76 in.
Weight:	34.76 lbs.
Speed:	Mach 2
Range:	3.12 miles
Altitude:	15,750 ft.

SS-1 Scud

SS-1 Scud Short-Range Ballistic Missile System—Iraq

It is a curious fact that a relatively obsolete missile, carrying moderate-sized warheads with imprecise accuracy, has proved to be an important weapon in the Persian Gulf war—at least from a political, if not a military, standpoint.

Intelligence reports vary, but Iraq was supposed to have had as many as 1,000 of the liquid-fueled Scuds prior to the outbreak of the war. Most were intended to be fired from fixed locations, although many were launched from mobile platforms as well.

Political and psychological damage

Aside from some minor damage, Scud attacks on Allied bases in Saudi Arabia were rendered ineffective by the U.S. Army's superb Patriot missile. Likewise, the physical harm inflicted on Israeli targets by initial Scud attacks was negligible. But the political and psychological damage they caused was certainly considerable.

The Scud can trace its history to the mid-1960s, when they began to enter service in the Soviet Union. Scuds were first mounted on tank chassis, then on modern carriers with fair cross-country mobility. The missile was originally designed to carry a 100-kiloton nuclear warhead or a 2,000-pound conventional warhead, with ranges varying from 100 miles to 175 miles, respectively. The principal Iraqi threat lay in the use of warheads containing chemical or biological agents.

The first combat use of the Scud occurred in 1973 during the Arab-Israeli Yom Kippur war; it was later used in

Artist's conception of a Scud lifting off from a fixed site.

indiscriminate attacks against Iranian cities in the Iran-Iraq war.

The most dangerous Scuds are the mobile versions, which have a fully amphibious transporter-erector-launcher. A considerable portion of the United Nations' air effort in Operation Desert Storm was directed toward the elimination of the mobile Scuds.

One U.S. military spokesman, commenting on the difficulty of locating mobile Scud launchers during Operation Desert Storm, remarked that it was like trying to find "a single flatbed truck in Texas."

SS-1 SCUD SHORT-RANGE BALLISTIC MISSILE

Length:	19 ft., 8 in.
Weight:	6,614 lbs. at launch
Guidance:	Inertial
Warhead:	100-kt nuclear or 1,802-lb. conventional
Range:	175 miles

Frog-7, Al-Hussein, Al-Abbas, Silkworm, and SA-6 Missiles
—Iraq

A trio of Frog-7 missiles on mobile launchers maneuver for position in the Soviet Union's Carpathian Military District. Like the Scud, this obsolete missile's usefulness is limited primarily to its value as a terror weapon.

Iraq disposes of a wide variety of missiles in addition to the Scud. The Al-Hussein and the Al-Abbas are modified Scud surface-to-surface missiles. Their ranges have been increased to 375 miles and 575 miles, respectively, by reducing warhead size. Both missiles purportedly have the capability to deliver chemical and biological agents. However, their increased range has served to diminish basic reliability and accuracy.

The Iraqis also have a smaller number of the Frog-7 surface-to-surface missiles. The Frog-7 has a single solid-propellant rocket providing the thrust necessary to throw a 990-pound chemical warhead up to 37 miles.

An unsophisticated weapon

Communist China has made a fortune selling their Silkworm missiles to various countries throughout the world. Primarily intended as an antiship missile, the Silkworm can be fired from surface installations or dropped from bombers. They are unsophisticated weapons, with stubby delta wings and tail—near copies of the Soviet SS-N-2 Styx. A booster rocket is jettisoned after take-off, and another rocket sustains the speed at .8 Mach. The Silkworm carries an 882-pound conventional warhead, and has a range of 26 miles.

Iraq also posesses a number of SA-6 Gainful surface-to-air missiles. The SA-6 is remembered for the havoc it wreaked against Israeli aircraft during the 1973 Yom Kippur war. The SA-6 has a range of 37 miles and carries a 176-pound conventional warhead. Although its effectiveness is mitigated by advances in electronic countermeasures, it remains a mobile system with a Strait Flush radar system for guidance.

FROG 7, SILKWORM, AND SA-6 MISSILES

	Frog-7	Silkworm	SA-6
Length:	29 ft., 6 in.	20 ft., 6 in.	20 ft., 4 in.
Weight:	5,511 lbs.	5,000 lbs.	1,213 lbs.
Guidance:	Radio command	Radar/infrared	Radar-tracked
Warhead:	990 lbs.	882 lbs.	176 lbs.
Range:	37 miles	26 miles	37 miles

Chemical and Biological Warfare
—Iraq

A Marine instructor adjusts a gas mask on a trainee. Once a distant memory of the First World War, the specter of chemical warfare has recently returned to haunt modern-day battlefields.

Poison gas warfare is dangerous to all involved. All it takes is a sudden shift in the wind to turn a cloud of drifting gas into a wanton killer of friend and foe alike. Similarly, biological agents can be perilously fickle: A fatal disease, once unleashed, does not recognize boundaries between armies, or nations.

Saddam Hussein has often been compared, usually unfavorably, with Adolf Hitler. During most of World War II the Nazi dictator also had at his disposal large quantities of poison gas, and he had studied position papers on the biological warfare option. Yet even at the end, with his world crashing down around him, Hitler refrained from using either chemical or biological agents. One can only speculate that, having himself been gassed during the First World War, Hitler hated such weapons with a passion that mitigated against their use.

The Iraqi ruler never had the benefit of Hitler's experience with gas. Nor did he hesitate to use gas when it suited his purposes to do so. At Hussein's orders, the Iraqi armed forces employed gas indiscriminately against both the Iranian population and the Kurdish minority within Iraq.

A tricky proposition
The use of poison gas is an inherently tricky proposition. Nevertheless, prior to the invasion of Kuwait, Iraq had stockpiled almost 1,500 tons of mustard gas—the terror of the First World War. Mustard gas is a blistering agent; if inhaled, it blisters the lungs and breathing becomes an agony. More formidable, and deadly, were Iraq's nerve gases—Tabun, Sarin, and

VX. A single droplet of nerve gas on exposed skin can cause death within ten minutes.

As Operation Desert Storm got underway, the anticipation of chemical weapons caused almost as much discomfort and psychological harm as their actual use. Scud missile alerts forced troops to don functional cumbersome protective clothing. Meanwhile, the civilian population of Israel was held hostage by the threat. Not only were Israeli civilians compelled to keep their gas masks close at the ready, they also had to seek refuge in the oppressive sanctuary of sealed rooms. The confused pattern of Scud alarms, both real and false, served to set nerves on edge— which may have been Hussein's ultimate goal.

SEA WEAPONRY

As Operation Desert Shield/ Desert Storm geared up, the United States Navy strengthened its contingent of ships already in the Middle East. Aircraft carriers, battleships, cruisers, destroyers, frigates, and numerous support ships were all deployed to the Persian Gulf, the Red Sea, and the Mediterranean Sea. Since Iraq had a very small and ineffective navy, allied forces essentially controlled the waves.

The Persian Gulf campaign brought about one event that no expert would have predicted —the reemergence of the battleship as an important element in combat. However, the battleship's 16-inch guns were not the dominant weapon. Instead, the accurate Tomahawk cruise missile—operated against targets considered too dangerous for manned aircraft— proved effective and lethal. Other naval vessels, including cruisers and frigates, also fired Tomahawk missiles, as well as providing escort duty.

Aircraft carriers' fighter jets, attack planes, and other aircraft supplemented the fighting

Aging symbol of American naval power, the World War II-era battleship Missouri (BB 62) *has proved in the Persian Gulf that it remains a formidable weapon of war.*

power of allied air forces. Self-contained, not intruding on the local economy or customs, aircraft carriers proved their worth once and for all.

The sea task force of the United Nations may be a decisive element in an allied victory, supporting both the air and land forces against Iraq.

Aircraft Carriers

Aircraft Carriers—United States

The aircraft carriers of the United States Navy are the largest and most powerful surface warships ever built. When at sea, they lead heavily armed squadrons of fighting and support ships in units called battle groups. These mighty ships come in six distinct classes, of which two—*Enterprise* and *Nimitz*—are nuclear-powered. The carriers of the *Midway, Forrestal, Kitty Hawk,* and *Kennedy* classes are all conventionally powered.

Carrier aircraft attack

The United States Navy perfected the art of carrier warfare during World War II. Since then, U.S. carriers have participated in conflicts ranging from Southeast Asia to Central America, from the Mediterranean to the Persian Gulf. In Operation Desert Storm, U.S. carrier aircraft struck hard and often at Iraqi military assets. The carriers were also charged with the defense of allied shipping and ground forces.

The U.S. Navy deployed the following carriers in the Red Sea, the Persian Gulf, and the Mediterranean Sea for Operation Desert Storm: The *Midway* (*Midway* class); the *Saratoga, America,* and *Ranger* (*Forrestal* class); the *John F. Kennedy* (*Kennedy* class); and the *Theodore Roosevelt* (*Nimitz* class). The *Forrestal* was dispatched to the eastern Mediterranean.

The *Nimitz*-class ships, profiled here, are the Navy's largest and most modern carriers. They typically carry about 86 aircraft, including two fighter squadrons totaling 20 F-14 Tomcats; two strike-fighter squadrons totaling 20 F/A-18

The USS Eisenhower *(CVN 69), a nuclear-powered* Nimitz-*class carrier, has an offensive armament exceeded in power only by the Navy's nuclear submarines.*

Hornets; and two attack squadrons totaling ten A-6E Intruders. The remaining aircraft, both fixed wing and rotary (helicopter), are used for electronic warfare, airborne early warning, and antisubmarine warfare.

In an awesome display of seapower, the U.S. Navy deployed six carrier battle groups to the Mideast. The oldest carrier—the *Midway*—was commissioned in 1945. The newest is the *Theodore Roosevelt,* commissioned in 1986.

NIMITZ-CLASS (CVN) AIRCRAFT CARRIERS

Displacement:	81,600 tons
Dimensions:	
Length overall:	1,089 ft.
Beam:	134 ft.
Draft:	37 to 38 ft., 6 in.
Speed:	30 knots (34.5 mph)
Aircraft:	F-14 Tomcats, F/A-18 Hornets, A-7E Corsair IIs, A-6E Intruders, EA-6B Prowlers, E-2C Hawkeyes, S-3A Vikings, SH-3H Sea Kings or SH-60 Sea Hawks

Battleships

Battleships—United States

The battleship USS Missouri *(BB 63), displays its mighty arsenal of 16-inch guns. In Operation Desert Storm, the* Missouri *and its sister ship* Wisconsin *(BB 64) were extraordinarily effective as Tomahawk cruise missile launching platforms.*

Completed in 1943 and 1944, *Iowa*-class battleships were the last ships of their kind to enter Navy service. Moreover, they remain the only battleships in active service with any of the world's navies. As the center-piece of task forces called surface action groups (SAG), battleships serve as fire support ships and missile-launching platforms for proximate air, sea, and ground operations.

In March 1983, the *New Jersey* became the second ship in the U.S. Navy to receive the Tomahawk cruise missile. Along with the Harpoon antiship missile, Tomahawk land-attack and antiship missiles now constitute the main armament of *Iowa*-class battleships. The installation of missiles has not come at the expense of tradi-tional heavy guns, however. All *Iowa* ships still retain three turrets holding a total of 12 16-inch guns, and six five-inch turrets totaling 12 guns.

A new lease on life

In effect, modern missile technology has given the battle-ship a new lease on life. While not as versatile as aircraft carriers, missile-armed *Iowa*-class battleships are still capable of playing an important role in American military strategy, as events in the Persian Gulf war demonstrated. Many naval experts also contend that the battleships' big guns could, in certain situations, prove more useful than missiles against enemy surface threats and more efficient than aircraft for shore bombardment missions.

In 1987, the *Missouri* served as part of a multinational task force that was sent into the Persian Gulf to protect merchant shipping during the Iran-Iraq war. The *Missouri* was subse-quently joined by the *Wisconsin* prior to the outbreak of hostilities with Iraq. In Operation Desert Storm, the *Missouri* and *Wisconsin* both launched Tomahawk missiles at Iraqi targets with extreme accuracy and effectiveness.

IOWA-CLASS (BB) BATTLESHIPS

Displacement:	57,350 tons
Dimensions:	
Length:	887 ft., 3 in.
Beam:	108 ft., 2.4 in.
Draft:	38 ft.
Speed:	33 knots (37.95 mph)
Armament:	Sixteen Harpoon SSMs
	Thirty-two Tomahawk sea- and land-attack cruise missiles
	Nine 16-inch Mk 7 guns
	Twelve 5-inch dual-purpose Mk 28 guns
	Four 20mm Phalanx CIWS guns

Cruisers
Cruisers—United States

Cruisers have long been the naval mainstay of all great maritime powers. They were originally designed to act alone as powerfully armed ships or to lead squadrons of smaller warships. During World War II, U.S. cruisers became the "utility ships" of the Navy, a role that involved them in the majority of ship-to-ship engagements.

The 33 cruisers now in service are divided into eight classes; nine of the 33 are nuclear-powered, and the rest are powered by conventional means. Thirteen cruisers are equipped with five-inch guns, and ten cruisers have no guns at all except for air-defense guns.

Antiaircraft escorts
Like the cruisers of yesteryear, these newer ships serve as antiaircraft escorts for task forces headed by aircraft carriers. All are fitted with surface-to-air missiles and Harpoon antiship missiles. Some are fitted with Tomahawk land-attack and antiship cruise missiles and vertical launch missiles such as the ASROC (Anti-Submarine Rocket). The cruiser force supports aircraft carrier battle groups and battleship-led surface action groups.

Thirteen cruisers are now under construction. The high cost of nuclear power plants and related equipment, coupled with improvements in super-power relations, makes it unlikely that any more nuclear-powered cruisers will be built.

Ten U.S. cruisers participated in Operation Desert Storm. The most modern ships in this class, profiled here, are the *Ticonderoga* cruisers. Equipped with a sophisticated Aegis radar and fire control system and armed with numerous surface-to-air missiles, *Ticonderoga*-

class cruisers are well suited to carry out their primary mission of task force air defense. Sixteen cruisers in this class are armed with Tomahawk cruise missiles for offensive operations.

Cruisers like the Ticonderoga-*class* Bunker Hill *(CG 52) are charged with the task of protecting battleships and carriers from air attack by bombers and antiship missiles.*

TICONDEROGA-CLASS (CG) GUIDED-MISSILE CRUISERS

Displacement:	9,400 to 9,530 tons
Dimensions:	
Length:	565 ft.
Beam:	55 ft.
Draft:	31 ft., 6 in.
Speed:	30 + knots (34.5 mph)
Armament:	Harpoon missiles; 12.75-inch torpedoes; Mk 45 guns; 20mm Phalanx CIWS guns; Standard-MR missiles; ASROC launchers; Tomahawk missiles
Fire control:	Mk 7 Aegis; Mk 86 fire control system; Mk 99 missile directors; Mk 116 fire control system; Tomahawk fire control system

Destroyers

Destroyers—United States

The USS Spruance *(DD 963) is the name-ship of the United States Navy's largest destroyer class.*

Ships known as destroyers saw their first major action during the Russo-Japanese War (1904-05). As originally conceived, they were to be torpedo carriers whose targets were armored cruisers and battleships. World War I and World War II saw a steady decline in the use of destroyers as torpedo-firing warships against other warships. Among the Allies in particular, a new role for the destroyer emerged: convoy escort and antisubmarine vessel.

Firepower equal to a WWII task force

Since the end of World War II, the destroyer's weight and armament have changed, and so has the definition of a destroyer's duties. Early on in the postwar era the guided missile proved to be more accurate and more destructive to enemy aircraft than the gun, and it quickly replaced the gun as the destroyer's main weapon. Guided missiles were also developed for antisubmarine and antiship warfare, as well as for land-based targets. Today, a missile-armed destroyer can pack the punch of an entire World War II task force, even without nuclear warheads.

The Navy currently deploys six destroyer classes totaling some 68 ships. About 37 of these are classified as guided-missile destroyers and are armed with surface-to-air missiles (SAMs). While the remaining destroyers may also carry SAMs, their primary concern is antisubmarine warfare. This is particularly true of the *Spruance*-class ships, which comprise the mainstay of the U.S. destroyer fleet. With their large hulls and block structures, *Spruance* destroyers endured heavy criticism; they did not fit the cut and thrust greyhound image of the past. Rather, *Spruance* ships are designed to allow continuous updating of the weapons systems. *Spruance* destroyers, profiled here, are the most heavily armed destroyers among the world's navies.

SPRUANCE-CLASS (DD) DESTROYERS

Displacement:	8,040 tons
Dimensions:	
Length:	529 ft.
Beam:	55 ft.
Draft:	29 ft.
Speed:	32.5 knots (37.4 mph)
Armament:	Sea Sparrow missiles; Harpoon missiles; 12.75-inch torpedoes; 20mm Phalanx CIWS guns; Mk 45 guns; Tomahawk missiles; ASROC missiles
Fire control:	Tomahawk fire control system; Mk 91 missile control system; Mk 86 fire control system; Mk 116 fire control system

Frigates
Frigates—United States

Frigates were originally two-decked sailing ships that carried their armament on the top deck only. Among the more famous of the sail-powered frigates is the *Constitution* (otherwise known as Old Ironsides), which is still in commission and berthed in Boston Harbor. The demise of sail-powered warships in the mid- to late-1800s resulted in the disappearance of frigates as well. With the coming of World War II, however, the frigate designation was revived in the U.S. Navy.

The concept of the frigate has remained constant over the years—a small, relatively inexpensive vessel that is swift enough to carry out escort duties. Today, all Navy frigates are antisubmarine warfare escorts. *Oliver Hazard Perry*-class frigates also provide limited anti-air warfare (AAW) protection. The Navy currently has 98 frigates, with 19 more in the Naval Reserve fleet. The 19 Reserve ships have combined active and reserve crews. No frigates are under construction, and none are planned. Plans to build an advanced-design frigate were canceled in 1986.

Largest ship class in the Navy

The *Oliver Hazard Perry*-class of frigates, profiled here, contains 51 ships, making it the largest single ship class in the U.S. Navy. These ships are armed with torpedoes, surface-to-air and antiship missiles, and a 75 millimeter rapid-firing cannon. But their two anti-submarine warfare helicopters (housed in twin adjacent hangars at the rear of the superstructure) constitute their main armament. Like the destroyers of the *Spruance* class, *Oliver Hazard Perry* ships are propelled by

gas turbine engines that enable them to attain a top speed of at least 28 knots.

The U.S. Navy deployed six frigates in the naval component of Operation Desert Storm. Like the destroyers, they were charged with escort duties for battleship surface action groups and aircraft carrier battle groups.

Although designed primarily as antisubmarine warfare escorts, Oliver Hazard Perry-class frigates like the USS Estocin *(FFG 15) provide limited anti-air warfare (AAW) protection as well.*

OLIVER HAZARD PERRY-CLASS (FFG) GUIDED-MISSILE FRIGATES

Displacement:	3,650 tons
Dimensions:	
Length:	445 ft. or 453 ft.
Beam:	45 ft.
Draft:	24 ft., 6 in.
Speed:	28+ knots (32.2+ mph)
Armament:	Standard-MR or Harpoon missiles; 12.75-inch torpedoes; Mk 75 gun; 20mm Phalanx CIWS gun
Fire control:	Mk 13 weapon director; Mk 92 fire control system; STIR radar

Cruise Missiles

Cruise Missiles—United States

The battleship New Jersey *(BB 62) fires off a Tomahawk cruise missile. Tomahawks launched from the* New Jersey's *sister ships,* Missouri *(BB 63) and* Wisconsin *(BB 64), wreaked havoc on Saddam Hussein's war machine.*

The BGM-109 Tomahawk Land Attack Missile (TLAM) was developed by General Dynamics for use by both surface ships and submarines. The TLAM-N has a 200-kiloton nuclear warhead; the TLAM-C and TLAM-D have conventional warheads with 1,000 pounds of high explosives and submunitions, respectively. All three TLAM variants have a range of nearly 1,400 miles. A second Tomahawk variation is the Tomahawk Antiship Missile (TASM), which is designed for use against surface ships. The TASM has a 1,000-pound conventional warhead and a range of 285 miles.

Unique guidance system

The TLAM uses an inertial guidance system with a unique pattern matching system that compares the features of the surface terrain passing beneath the missile with a map stored in its computer. This enables the TLAM to fly at low altitudes, thus eluding enemy radar detection. The TASM does not have the terrain-following system, which is unnecessary for over-the-water flight. All Tomahawks have a subsonic maximum speed of approximately 500 miles per hour.

The AGM-86B air-launched cruise missile (ALCM) is launched from B-52G and B-52H Stratofortress bombers and FB-111 Aardvark bombers. The ALCM is similar in design and performance to the TLAM and TASM series of missiles.

The TLAM and the TASM are fitted on *Iowa*-class battleships; cruisers of the *Virginia, Long Beach,* and *Ticonderoga* classes; and destroyers of the *Arleigh Burke* and *Spruance* classes. Some of these ships fire their Tomahawks from armored box launchers that serve as storage and launch containers, but most fire the missiles from vertical launchers. Tomahawks can also be fired from 21-inch submarine torpedo tubes and, in the later *Los Angeles*-class attack submarines, from vertical launch tubes.

Literally within the first few minutes of Operation Desert Storm, Tomahawk missiles launched from the battleships *Missouri* and *Wisconsin* struck with astonishing accuracy at Iraqi command centers, radar installations, and other military assets.

TOMAHAWK CRUISE MISSILE

Length:	20 ft., 5 in.
Diameter:	1 ft., 7 in.
Weight:	3,290 lbs.
Speed:	548 mph
Range:	552 miles
Warhead:	200-kt nuclear or 264-lb. high-explosive